The Life-Savers

Rhode Island's Forgotten Service

Nice to meet you and enjoyed our discussions

The Life-Savers
Rhode Island's Forgotten Service

Varoujan Karentz

The Life-Savers

Rhode Island's Forgotten Service

All rights reserved © 2012 by Varoujan Karentz

No part of this book may be used or transmitted in any form or by any means, graphic, electronic or mechanical including photocopying, recording or taping by any informational retrieving system without the written permission of the publisher or author.

CreateSpace
7290 B. Investment Drive
Charleston, SC 29418
U.S.A.

Printed in U.S.A.

ISBN-13: 978-1463791025
ISBN-10: 146379102X

Cover design by Author
Images NOAA & U.S. Coast Guard Files

Contents

Forward vii

Acknowledgements xi

Chapter 1   Maritime Growth and the Need
            to Save Lives 13

Chapter 2   The Service 29

Chapter 3   The Rhode Island Stations 63

Chapter 4   The Block Island Stations 79

Chapter 5   Watch Hill Station 123

Chapter 6   Narragansett Pier Station 149

Chapter 7   Brenton Point Station 163

Chapter 8   Point Judith Station 183

Chapter 9   Quonochontaug Station 215

Chapter 10 Green Hill Station 233

Chapter 11 The Rhode Island Volunteer
            Life-Saving Service 239

Bibliography 251

Foreword

This book covers the history of one of Rhode Island's forgotten maritime services, the U.S. Life-Saving Service. The service consisted of manned stations linked as a chain of coastal seaward sentinels established for one purpose - to save lives. When most of us think of life-saving at sea or in our harbors, visions of U.S. Coast Guard (*Semper Paratus*) cutters and helicopters come to mind. What preceded them in 1915 was a heroic service of hearty men and hundreds of life-saving stations folded into that force we know today. Organizationally, they were a string of sentinels along the nation's coastline with men walking the beaches and looking for ships in distress or stranded perilously on rocks and shoals along our shorelines. This string of guardians stretched over parts of the eastern seaboard, the Gulf of Mexico, the Great Lakes, and western shores including Alaska.

For over sixty years, men from nine Rhode Island U.S. Life-Saving Stations monitored the southern Rhode Island coastline and Block Island, often performing heroic feats with little regard for their own safety. Their motto, *"You have to go out, but you don't have to come back."* was instilled in each crewmember. They started out as volunteers and were gradually recruited into government service. The stations grew with America's commitment to saving the lives of those involved in marine disasters. As part of a nation-wide establishment of coastal stations, their duties (with very few exceptions) would take place when the sea and surf was in

Foreword

turmoil with treacherous waves and white water pulsed by screeching gale force winds. Few know their remarkable feats of heroism.

My first introduction to the rigors of these "surfmen" as they were called, was during World War II when I was a 17-year old Coast Guard recruit at boot camp training in Sheepshead Bay, Manhattan Beach, NY. I earned a rower's seat on a gleaming white 36-ft surfboat and raced against other surfboats. My instructor coxswain was the training base Athletic Development Director, *Bibber McCoy*, a professional wrestler in civilian life under the direction of the famous boxer *Lt. Jack Dempsey*. *McCoy* had little sympathy for members of our boat crew. He drove us to the verge of collapse, over and over again. Our fingers blistered and bled, our arms and backs ached, and the calluses of our hands and seat bottoms never healed from the excruciating rowing of the 1,000-lb surfboat. While we won few races during our training period, the memories of the rigors of the surfboat crew race training never left me. It was 65 years later that the importance of these life-saving stations sparked my interest. Remembering my boot camp rowing experiences, I fully realized and appreciated the difficulties surfmen endured. Their experiences were not like mine in the calm waters at boot camp, but rather having to launch a boat under horrific winter weather conditions in breaking surf and rowing out to sea.

While the story of the U.S. Life-Saving Service is often referred to as the "lost service", the works of recent authors as well as government documents exist describing details of how the service responded to shipwrecks. This book is not

Foreword

intended to replicate or document historical facts, or be used as a technical journal or an encyclopedic reference. Rather, its purpose is to highlight the role of Rhode Island's Life-Saving Stations and the men who staffed them. This book describes how they contributed to saving lives in an era when unusual feats of heroism were under taken by so few in such unimaginable conditions.

The chapters in this book will enlighten the reader of the Rhode Island Life-Saving Stations, their locations, the station crews, how they lived, and how and why they went to sea or patrolled the beaches looking for ships in distress. Winter months were dark, bleak and cold, yet time after time, saving a life rewarded their diligence.

Nationwide thousands of incidents were reported and thousands of lives saved by the Service. Historians, including the U.S. Coast Guard who took over the Service in 1915, have documented the Life-Saving Service's remarkable history in various forms. However, Rhode Island events have never previously been consolidated into one book. While this book attempts to do that, it mainly highlights some of the more significant disasters that took place where surfmen were called upon to provide assistance to disabled vessels and those that were in distress. It also acknowledges some of the mundane tasks that were handily accomplished with little or no fanfare.

Many of the events and incidents at the Rhode Island Stations recorded in this book are direct quotations and excerpts from the annual U.S. Life-Saving Service reports. These reports cover a 39-year period from 1877 to 1916. The reader should understand that many of the reports are terse and lacking details or descriptive narrative because they were written by the surfmen in the station log. Unfortunately, paper and ink were not supplied in quantity, nor was writing their forte. These men lacked the vivid eloquent literary skills to describe the excitement of the rescues and of the difficult conditions under which many of the events took place. It is up to the reader to visualize the enormous burdens and physical challenges these men endured, almost always in gale force wind conditions coupled with horrendous breaking surf and seas.

Dennis Noble in his book *That Others May Live,* points out that many of these surfmen were perhaps "laconic" and could not express themselves in their log writings. The men were simply doing their duty and "believed in the traditional sailors' effort to help another sailor in distress".

Coupled with the U.S. Life-Saving Service, a second Rhode Island organization, the Rhode Island Volunteer Life-Saving Service, paralleled their activities. While this state service did not reflect the drama of the coastal stations, the Rhode Island Volunteer Life-Saving Service was also formed to save lives. It would be remiss if it were not included in this writing. Accordingly, a chapter in this book is devoted exclusively to them and their dedication and preparedness to saving the lives of Rhode Islanders on the inland lakes and ocean beaches.

Acknowledgments

In writing any historical essay, the author relies on many sources of material and the content of the book is based on records, images and recollections. In this case a very high percentage of information was obtained from the official records of the U.S. Life-Saving Service (LSS) and noted authors who had previously written and published works on the LSS. To them I owe thanks for their diligence and the opportunity to learn much about the Service from their publications.

In addition to all the source material, this work required reading and research of thirty-nine book-size annual reports, selection of information, and transcription by extracting data related to the Rhode Island stations. It was coupled with the help of the following people and organizations who I wish to thank for their time, patience, tolerance and guidance.

To both my daughters, Deneb Karentz and Sona Andrews, both career scholars, for their editorial reviews and comments. Deneb's manuscript reviews were done while on assignment at remote Palmer Station in Antarctica during the Antarctic winter. James Jenney, Beavertail Lighthouse Museum Association's shipwreck historian corrected, contributed and commented on specific shipwrecks from his vast knowledge and archives of Rhode Island shipwrecks. Richard Sullivan led me to sources of information at Mystic Seaport and sites along the Rhode Island south shore. LCDR "Bud" Cooney, USCG (ret) first introduced me to the existence of the LSS. The National U.S. Life-Saving Service

Acknowledgements

Heritage Association and their repository of documents and photos provided a great deal of information. The U.S. Coast Guard historian's office and their Groton, Connecticut library/museum have preserved a wealth of historic content about their inherited service. The U.S. National Archives Records Center in Waltham, Massachusetts for access to their vast collection of station logs, letters and reports. And the Beavertail Lighthouse Museum Association, who through my affiliation, opened many doors to other organizations I contacted for help and information.

Chapter One

Maritime Growth and the Need to Save Lives

Life-Saving Today

Today, life-saving is almost automatic. While still perilous, it is a far cry from surfmen pulling the oars of an open boat in breaking waves. *William Sisson,* editor of *Soundings* magazine, best describes today's scenario:

> *"In the Atlantic a 31–foot trimaran battered by a series of gales begins to break up, losing parts of the boat. With the vessel in danger of sinking, the stricken sailor triggers the red button on his DSC VHF radio. A 607-foot tanker within range of his radio signal diverts to the trouble spot, arrives on the scene and the crew hauls the lucky seaman aboard."*

and

> *"A team of four Air National Guardsman from a SAR (Search and Rescue) Wing parachute in the night with an inflatable boat to provide medical assistance to a sailor who has suffered a head injury."*

> *"All in the day's work they say."*

That is the daily work of the U.S. Coast Guard, the agency that inherited the early Life-Saving Service, turning Beach Patrol into Search and Rescue (SAR) wherever the location.

1 Maritime Growth

In either the case of yesteryear or today, as *Sisson* describes, "it is heroism built into the job."

By far, today, the largest workload related to saving lives along our shores and out at sea involves recreational boating. There are over 11 million boats registered nationwide, and each summer the Coast Guard is kept busy responding to Mayday calls. No such technology existed in the 19th century, but the need and human compassion to save lives was the same.

During the period 1875 to 1904 the average number of lives lost to shipwrecks stranding along U.S. shores was 250 to 350 per year. Between 1903 and 1904, 1,281 lives were lost.

This book traces the start of the Life-Saving Service where a chain of men, almost hand in hand, patrolled thousands of miles of America's coastline. The book specifically focuses on the locations and events of the Life-Saving Service in Rhode Island, like-minded men who wanted to save lives. They strived often to do so, yet from time to time lost the battle to the sea. They were a tough team of men with crude equipment who did their best for over a half century and have almost been forgotten. The demise of these life-saving stations was the direct result of the evolution in transportation taking place at the turn of the 19th century. Railroads and motor transportation on improved roads and highways were rapidly replacing the coastwise trade of cargo and passenger service by slow boats, packets and schooners. At the same time, newly developed steam and fueled engines were giving vessels greater maneuverability and resulting in far fewer marine disasters. By the 1930s,

Life-Saving Stations were being closed throughout the country.

By that time, the U.S. Coast Guard was established and took over the duties of the Life-Saving Service. As early as 1916 they were examining the advantages of aircraft for rescue operations, as an adjunct to their land and sea operations. As it turned out, airborne SAR has become a major strong arm of the Coast Guard rescue service.

> *1916 excerpt from the U.S. Coast Guard Annual Report examining the value of aircraft use for life-saving purposes:*
>
> **AVIATION.**
>
> In the saving of human life and property from the ravages of the elements, which is one of the principal functions of the Coast Guard, advantage should be taken of all new inventions and methods. Aviation has advanced to such a stage that air craft as now constructed and developed can be used most advantageously in activities of the Coast Guard. When a shipwreck occurs too far from the shore to be reached with the line-throwing gun, and the state of the sea makes it impossible to use the service boats, it is believed possible to carry a line to the wreck by means of an aeroplane, and thereby effect the rescue of persons who might otherwise perish. The finding of derelicts soon after they are first reported is of such vital importance, that their ultimate recovery and removal from the paths of commerce ofttimes depends entirely upon the rapidity with which they are definitely located. The value of aeroplanes in this connection has passed beyond the realm of speculation, and there is now no doubt that the use of air craft will greatly facilitate this important work by the Coast Guard. Anticipating that the Coast Guard must adopt this new method of life-saving as soon as practicable, three junior officers have already been assigned to undergo training at naval aviation and private schools in order to form the nucleus of a force trained for aviation purposes. The desirability of providing aviation stations and equipment for the Coast Guard has been represented to Congress, with the result that authority to undertake this additional function has been incorporated in the pending naval appropriation bill. Aside from the humanitarian possibilities of this proposition, the fact must not be overlooked that aviation facilities provided for the Coast Guard will be a valuable addition to naval aviation equipment in time of war.

1 Maritime Growth

Life-Saving Stations

During the period from 1872 through 1938 nine life-saving stations were operational at various times in Rhode Island. After 1938, only three sites remained and the U.S. Coast Guard now operates those under the modern role of Search and Rescue and Homeland Security.

The original need to establish life-saving stations was the result of the extraordinary levels and magnitude of shipping that took place during the 1800s as the country began its expansion both geographically and economically. Populations were centered at seaports and navigable coastal features primarily because of the efficient transport of large quantities of bulk goods that could be achieved by maritime shipping.

Lack of infrastructure, equipment, clearance of forests and construction of bridges hampered road and railway transportation. Water transportation of goods and people between ports grew at a rapid rate and along with it, more tall ships, sailing packets and the ever-famous wooden multi-masted schooners. By the mid-1800s steamships, or "steamers" as they were called, began appearing along America's coastlines and at the turn of that century they began to catch up and compete with the thousands of sailing vessels plying the coasts.

1 Maritime Growth

Excerpt from Annual U.S. Life-Saving Service Report 1879:

TABLE 7.—*Abstract of returns of disasters to vessels on the* ATLANTIC *and* GULF *coasts during the year ending June 30, 1879, showing the number of vessels and distinguishing their* DESCRIPTION.

Description of vessels.	July.	August.	September.	October.	November.	December.	January.	February.	March.	April.	May.	June.	Total.
Barges		1		3					3	1	1		9
Barks	2	2	3	3	2	2	7	5	5	1	1	2	34
Barkentines							1				1		2
Brigs	1		4	3	4	1	3	1	4	5	1	2	29
Brigantines						1	1	1					3
Canal-boats			1						1				2
Ferry-boats	1		3	2		2	2	1	1	2			13
Schooners	39	34	42	150	62	60	45	31	69	50	23	32	656
Scows	1	1				1							3
Ships				1	1		1		2	1			7
Sloops	4	2	1	10		1	4	2	2	1	4	3	34
Steamers	6	6	11	22	4	8	7	8	7	9	8	13	109
Steamships	3	4		3	2	3	5	2		1	2	5	30
Unknown	1		2		1	1							5
Total	58	50	66	196	77	81	76	53	92	80	50	57	936

Along with increase of maritime traffic, shipwrecks and other marine disasters also increased. Excluding the numbers of steamers that were entering the maritime trade, the variety of sailing vessels experiencing disasters were largely a function of size. The schooner, the workhorse of coastal commerce, was overwhelmingly predominant and as such was also in the forefront of occurring disasters.

In the 1800s, maritime traffic exceeded all other modes of transportation by orders of magnitude in the number of ships and passages. According to the 2010 Rhode Island Ocean Special Area Management Plan (Ocean SAMP), during the year 1893 more than 60,000 vessels passed Point Judith and over half of these (34,000) were coastal schooners. Even later, in 1917 when rail transportation had become prominent, Point Judith was seeing 70 to 100 vessels pass by each day. Within Narragansett Bay, keeper logbooks of

1 Maritime Growth

Passing Vessels at Beavertail Light Station recorded over 15,000 vessels per year.

Point Judith Passing Vessel Log 1917. Note that steamships had become more prominent than sailing vessels by this date.

```
Vessels Sighted from
   Station this day:
Ships    —
Barks    —
Brigs    —
Schooners    26
Steamers    35
Sloops    9
Barges in tow  1 8
```

Another stream of vessels outside the Point Judith avenue transited south and east of Block Island, adding thousands more to the count. This period was also the peak period of coal and thousands of towed coal barges transited Rhode Island's coastlines and Narragansett Bay. Many of these barges were converted from large multi-masted vessels that were no longer seaworthy under full sail.

Large sailing ships hampered by the inability to maneuver in gale force winds were forced to sail downwind and were unable to steer a course away from shoals and reefs. During the period 1875 to 1904 an average of 250 to 350 lives were lost per year by shipwrecks along America's shores. However, between 1903 and 1904 1,281 lives were lost and vessel strandings numbered in the thousands. As losses of vessels, cargo and lives escalated, the need for life-saving stations and equipment became critical. Hence, Rhode Island joined the other maritime states and the federal government's initiative to save lives of seamen in jeopardy.

1 Maritime Growth

Much has changed over the past 150 years in regard to the mechanics and methods of life-saving and the ethics of the sea. Heroism and its humanitarian application toward saving lives still engages the determination and will of those who venture into dangerous waters, often placing their lives in danger while trying to save others. It is a compassionate business with absolutely no material reward other than the thanks from those who are in peril. In the case of the infant U.S. Life-Saving Service in the mid- to late 1800s, the volunteers were initially unpaid, understaffed and ill equipped; yet they willingly placed their own lives in danger to save people they never knew. These events played out mostly along the shores and beaches of America as ships foundered (sunk), or were stranded (went aground) and broken apart from pounding on shoals, rocks or surf. Ships, cargo and lives were both lost and saved as each horrific event took place. The stories are epic and as disaster statistics rose each year, this force of visionary men built an organization, found new ways and new tactics, and maintained a continued determination to save lives. The stories of the men manning the Life-Saving Stations and patrolling beaches are heroic indeed and their fortitude, most always in inclement weather, was unbelievable, event after event. Communications and navigation tools slowly evolved; but it took a century and then decades, until improvements in technology minimized the need of men patrolling beaches looking for stranded vessels and breeching the onslaught of surf and sea to save lives.

Annual statistics of vessels rendered assistance, value of cargos and number of lives saved were meticulously recorded, complied and printed by the U.S. Life-Saving

Service, and later by the U.S. Coast Guard. However, these reports do not represent the full scale of rescues made.

Salvage companies, wrecking tugs and sea-going good Samaritans (those that took risks and saved ships and crews as an unwritten rule to help another sailor) are a few examples of others who played a contributing role in saving lives. Beginning in 1895, the Life-Saving Service published periodically in its annual report the following statement:

> "It is manifestly impossible to apportion the relative results accomplished. It is equally impossible to give even an approximate estimate of the number of lives saved by the station crews. It would be preposterous to assume that all those on board vessels suffering disaster who escape would have been lost but for the aid of the life-savers; yet the number of persons taken ashore by the lifeboats and other appliances by no means indicates the sum total saved by the Service. In many instances where vessels are released from stranding or other perilous predicaments by the lifesaving crews, both the vessels and those on board are saved, although the people are not actually taken ashore, and frequently the vessels and crews, escaping disaster entirely, are undoubtedly saved by the warning signals of the patrolmen, while in numerous cases, either where vessels suffer actual disaster or where they are only warned from danger, no loss of life would have ensued if no aid had been rendered."

The Nine Rhode Island Life-Saving Stations

Block Island
    Block Island Station
    New Shoreham Station
    Sandy Point Station

Block Island Sound and Rhode Island Sound
    Watch Hill Station
    Quonochontaug Station
    Green Hill Station
    Point Judith Station

Narragansett Bay
    Narragansett Pier Station
    Brenton Point Station

Divers and shipwreck historians often state that Rhode Island has experienced more shipwrecks that any other state in America. Known wrecks number over 1,000 and estimates range anywhere from 2,000 to 2,500. Some remains date back hundreds of years, such as the transport ships scuttled by the British in Newport Harbor during the Revolutionary War. What is not known nor estimated, are those ships that stranded (ran aground) and survived by floating off or being pulled off by tugs or their own winches and kedged anchors; or the others who avoided peril by being warned of dangers by lighthouses and the Life-Saving Service beach patrols who waved off vessels approaching danger with their red Coston lanterns.

Imagine if you can, a lone surfman dressed in storm clothes, hat and knee-high boots, patrolling a segment of beach in the middle of the night buffeted by wind, rain or snow. His only equipment would be a coil of rope, his patrol clock, a bevy of flares and his red signal lantern. With degraded visibility he sights a vessel approaching dangerously close to shore and waves his lantern to warn the crew of their impending doom. He is one man on the beach frantically trying to prevent a disaster. His fellow crewman are up to five miles away, asleep in their station knowing the beach patrol could very well summon them at any time. This simplistic surveillance system lasted four decades and is a rich, almost forgotten, legacy of Rhode Island's history.

The Larchmont Disaster

Disasters, shipwrecks and related rescues are understandably exciting. There were recurring and common along Rhode Island shores, and many are described in the following chapters. Those with loss of life are tragic. Major incidents that occurred during deplorable weather condition reflect the horrors of the sea and suffering of those who died. Not all occurred on local beaches. Some incidents took place outside the visual range of the Life-Saving Stations, further out to sea where help was needed and not available.

Rhode Island's most significant marine disaster, a collision between the 128-ft three-masted schooner *Harry P. Knowlton* and the Joy Line's 252-ft long passenger steamer the *Larchmont*, took place on the night of February 11, 1907. The *Larchmont* was a steam-powered side paddle wheeler on route from Providence to New York. It was holed off Watch Hill by the sailing schooner that was laden with 500 tons of coal. The *Knowlton* mistook the steamer's course and drove its bow into the port side of the steamer. The air temperature was -3° F and breaking seas and wind-driven spray froze to everything that was above water. The weight of the ice on both vessels made difficult steerage and crews had difficulty walking on deck.

The *Larchmont* sank within minutes of the collision. Neither vessel burned signals that could have been seen from shore. In the aftermath, hours later, a massive operation to rescue survivors and search for victims both dead and alive was set into motion. The "call to arms" collected rescue vessels from nearby the collision area and from afar. The *Harry Knowlton* unaware of the damage she caused to the *Larchmont* began to fill with water until she reached a point off Quonochontaug. Her crew put out in the schooner's lifeboat and rowed ashore. The strong northwest wind carried the remains of the *Larchmont*, her few survivors and the dead passengers and crew, the bodies frozen stiff, back toward Quonochontaug, Point Judith and Block Island.

While Rhode Island's Life-Saving Stations played no part in preventing the disastrous collision, nor saving passengers out at sea; they responded to save the few that made it to shore by providing clothing, food and shelter. The grimmer task was collecting the bodies of victims that washed up on the beaches.

Two days after the disaster, it was reported that 138 lives aboard the *Larchmont* were lost and only 17 survived. The actual count was never confirmed. Some death estimates were as high as 150 passengers and another 50 crewmembers. Some survivors came ashore on wreckage, others in boats, and one young man actually swam ashore. Frozen bodies, some with only nightgowns on and covered with ice and layers of salt spray, were recovered from ocean

1 Maritime Growth

waters and beaches. The dead bodies spread from Watch Hill to Narragansett and out to Block Island.

Surfmen from Rhode Island's life-saving stations responded without hesitation or concern for their own safety. The night was exceedingly cold, dark and stormy. The event occurred at 11:00 PM, ten miles northwest of Block Island and three miles southeast of Watch Hill. The collision was too far off shore for any of the four Life-Saving Stations along the south coast of Narragansett or the two stations on Block Island to see or be aware. The first news of the disaster came only after a single survivor by the name of *Fred Hiergsell* swam ashore after his lifeboat was swamped. He knocked on the window of the Block Island Lighthouse (North Light on Sandy Point) and the lighthouse keeper called the nearby Life-Saving Station. Keeper *Cat McVey* aroused his crew and alerted the surfmen on the other side of the island at the New Shoreham Station. Other passengers also arrived. Some lived, but most died. Bodies began to wash up on Sandy Point, and by noon the next day 40 bodies were recovered by the life-saving crew. The Life-Saving Service 1907 Annual Report states;

> *"Block Island's two life-saving stations, one at Sandy Point and the other at New Shoreham, were turned into morgues and hospitals during the night, and the dead crowded the living. The boat room floors were lined with the dead, each one frozen as stiff as the boards on which they rested. In the living and sleeping rooms the suffering survivors rested on cots and beds, racked with the pain of frozen limbs and shuddering with the recollection of the horror of their experiences. Many were denied the merciful*

unconsciousness of sleep, and throughout the long, dreary night they tossed and cried and sobbed, and the howling wind outside only served to keep fresh in their minds the terrors of the storm through which they had fought their way to the island. It is feared that none of those survivors will remain unscathed. The frost penetrated too deeply to be overcome by medical treatment and the surgeon's knife will be the only salvation of some of the unfortunates. Some will lose fingers, some hands, and it is feared some will be obliged to have limbs amputated."

Along the Narragansett shore at the Life-Saving Stations of Watch Hill, Quonochontaug, Green Hill and Narragansett, similar stories were told. As word of the disaster spread, hundreds of volunteers in addition to the Life-Saving Service surfmen looked for survivors and bodies along the beaches.

While no other single tragedy with loss of life as high as this has been repeated in Rhode Island waters, the preparedness of Rhode Island's Life-Saving Services in responding to a major disaster and saving those who came ashore was certainly demonstrated.

The Sea King Disaster

On January 26, 1895, twelve years before the *Larchmont* disaster, another event demonstrated the limitations of Life-Saving Station's services due to their inability to respond to events outside their visual horizon.

A large sea-going tug named *Sea King* had entered Block Island Sound from Long Island Sound towing five barges loaded with coal. The tug was bound for Providence when she began experiencing gale force winds and horrendous seas. By the time she was seven miles from Point Judith, seas were breaking over the vessel. Coupled with blinding snow, the visibility had deteriorated to the point where those on the tug could not see the length of the vessel. Around 2:00 AM the towline had parted and all five barges were adrift. (It was common practice to have crews aboard these large barges, many of which were older sailing vessels no long capable of sailing and were converted to coal carriers.) The barges were without propulsion or the ability to maneuver; they were at the mercy of the wind and breaking seas and no doubt were taking on water.

Two or three of the barges foundered and sank while the barge *American Eagle* stood by waiting for the opportunity to save members of the crew from the other barges. She too went under with the captain, his wife and deckhand, as did the barges *Bingee*, *Albert* and *Crocus*. The *Crocus* also had on board the captain, his wife, daughter and another crewmember. The tug *Sea King*, under difficult and hazardous conditions did succeed in saving the crew of the barge *Nellie*. In total twelve people (four women and eight men) lost their lives. Bodies of one man and one woman were found by the Quonochontaug beach patrol; other victims were discovered by the patrols from Point Judith.

Community Service

The chapters that follow highlight incidents involving dramatic rescues. However, the roles of the surfmen were not limited to walking the beaches, rowing out to stranded vessels and rescuing mariners in peril from rough seas. There were many day-to-day tasks that included a variety of seemingly odd and curious activities. These were logged and reported on a daily basis. Since each station was supplied with emergency food, clothing and medical supplies, they responded to the local community in any time of need. Most common were providing assistance to vessels dragging anchors who needed help in carrying out a kedge or picking up an anchor and resetting it. Surfmen often found small boats broken loose from their moorings that needed to be hauled up on a beach, or they assisted with launching a boat or helped to furl a sail. Surfmen were also called to action when passengers or crewmembers of passing vessels were brought ashore, or a lighthouse keeper needed to get out to his station in weather too rough for his small rowing skiff. Even pilots navigating a ship would signal the station to launch a boat to pick them up because the pilot boat was elsewhere. Resuscitation of local recreational swimmers often showed up in the logs because the surfmen were trained in techniques of handling a drowning victim. Other general tasks were providing assistance as needed to local police, fireman and the U.S. Lighthouse Service. At Block Island (Sandy Point), Watch Hill and Point Judith the lighthouses and the life-saving stations were adjacent to each other or nearby, which proved beneficial for cooperative help to both organizations in time of need.

Chapter Two
The Service

The U.S. Life-Saving Service, the "forgotten service", had its start in the United States first as a benevolent organization in Massachusetts named the Humane Society of the Commonwealth of Massachusetts. Organized in 1785, it foresaw the humanitarian need to help and assist mariners from shipwrecks along the outer shores of the state.

While the principle harbor of Boston, Massachusetts has access to the sea; it is still located behind a series of 30 barrier islands standing as far out as eight miles. The approach to Boston started ten miles out at sea and required navigating twisted channels around the outer harbor islands and its rocks and shoals, while at the same time calculating the rise and fall of 10-ft tides and associated currents. Being obedient to the direction of wind and its force, sailing any vessel without engine power required utmost navigation and ship handling skills. The larger the vessel, the more difficult it was to steer and the less responsive to the helm. Coupled with those variables, stormy weather made ship handling notoriously difficult and the results were strandings (running aground), foundering (sinking) and shipwrecks.

The Massachusetts Humane Society recognized that shipboard sailors, who were survivors of wrecks for whatever cause, could and often did find themselves ashore; so they began building small huts on Boston's outer islands and nearby shorelines. These huts were stocked with food, candles and kindling for building a fire for use by these survivors. While the concept and construction of these Humane Houses was admirable, the huts were often vandalized and looted of their contents, leaving survivors with only shelter. In addition, since boats were not provided there were no means to get to populated areas. By the early 1800s the idea of using crewed lifeboats rowed by men from a shore station was proven successful by the British, and later adopted by the Humane Society. In 1807 America's first lifeboat station was established in Cohasset, Massachusetts.

When a federal law mandated life-saving in 1848, the Watch Hill, Rhode Island station became one of the first, established in 1850. It was supplied with a metal surfboat, rockets, mortars, lanterns, shovels, ropes and other fundamental supplies.

For over 20 years the U.S. government provided equipment to facilities such as Watch Hill. Local communities were required to supply the volunteer manpower to save lives. It took more time and more disasters for the U.S. government to cede to the pressures of those concerned and institute a more formal organization.

In 1871 the Revenue Marine Bureau was re-established to manage both the existing life-saving stations and America's Revenue Cutter Service (in place since 1790). As broader responsibilities became apparent and the increase of ship disasters heightened public attention, on June 18, 1878 Congress passed an act to establish the U.S. Life-Saving Service as a separate organization for the purpose of saving lives. The Revenue Cutter Service was regulated to do the same, but on the high seas. (In January 1915 both services were combined and became to U.S. Coast Guard.) Congress authorized funding and a Board of Directors followed. Stations were established up and down the Eastern seaboard at intervals from four to seven miles apart and manned by "surfmen", who were mostly local men who understood their coastal area dangers, its tides and its currents. All were seamen who knew how to handle rowing boats in surf due to repeated training drills. Each station averaged six to seven surfmen plus a keeper who was in charge. They were hardy and fit enough to patrol the beaches, handle rescue apparatus, keep watch for vessels in distress and warn them if they were off course or heading for disaster. The seven-man team was ideal to man six oars and have a steersman (the station keeper) for the station's surfboat.

Pay was generally low, even by standards during the late 1800s. The service started paying surfmen $40 a month and by 1913 pay had increased to $65 a month for actual service. Part time surfmen were paid $3 per day for each occasion of service, not to exceed $10 per day when they provided service in a disaster. Keepers were paid $75 per month. On the Atlantic coast the surfmen were on duty for ten months a year. During June and July they were not paid. On the

Pacific coast service was a full time 12-month job and in the Great Lakes surfmen were employed about 8 months per year. While their only pay was formally from wages, they were not prohibited from receiving rewards from ship owners, masters or other persons who deemed their services were exemplary and deserving of gratuities.

The dangers and risks taken by the surfmen, particularly in surfboats, were directly proportional to the weather and surf conditions at the time of a rescue. The motto of *"You have to go out, but you don't have to come back."* often quoted and promulgated, did instill a level of fear among the life-saving crews. Often decisions made by the keeper to go or not to go into treacherous surf were difficult when trying to judge whose lives were in more danger, the stranded vessel or the life-saving crew. The Superintendent of the Life-Saving Service testified more than once that: "Frequently when a crew is going to a wreck, the men hand their watches out to bystanders, and leave messages as to the disposition of their property if they are drowned." Eighty percent of these men had families. Although they all wore cork life jackets, the danger of being swamped or capsized and having waves sweep over them would have the same effects as being submerged; not to mention the probability of freezing to death, which happened from time to time.

Shipwrecked survivors were immediately taken into the shelter of the Life-Saving Station where the station crew provided food, warmth, medical attention and dry clothes. Survivors were housed as long as necessary until they were physically able to be moved, or when transportation had been arranged to get them home. The Life-Saving Service paid the station crew, but gave no financial aid to shipwrecked people. Stepping up to this task and supplementing the services provided at the station was a national organization named the Blue Anchor Society, an association of women organized in 1880. It was formed for the purpose of extending aid to sick, injured and destitute persons rescued from shipwrecks and other situations of distress and danger. The women managed the organization and depended entirely on voluntary gifts. Some funds were raised from passengers on transatlantic steamers where volunteer entertainment was provided. Half of the contributions were given to the Seaman's Orphanage in Liverpool, England. The Blue Anchor Society advocated that the other half of the funds should be donated to their charity. This relief organization, headquartered in New York City, distributed boxes of clothing and blankets to the stations at no cost to the government.

In 1898, at the beginning of the demise of sailing vessels and the rapid replacement by steamships, the number of life-saving stations totaled 264. Of those, 192 were along the Atlantic and Gulf coasts, 56 on the Great Lakes, 15 along the Pacific Coast and one on the Ohio River in Kentucky. Eventually 279 stations were built along the entire East and Gulf coasts (200 stations), parts of Pacific Northwest (20 stations) including a station in Alaska, and along the shores of the Great Lakes (79 stations) where winter storms cause massive disasters and loss of life. By 1907, 1,898 surfmen were employed. The station crews lived on site with meager salaries, often located along remote strands of beaches and marshlands. During the off season months of July and August surfmen resorted to better paying jobs such as fishing, running pleasure boats and driving teams for summer people at the beaches.

By 1908 serious deficiencies in staffing due to physical disabilities and pay caused enough concern that a special congressional hearing was called to listen to Service complainants and to find ways to remedy the enrollment problem. Over 500 job vacancies existed. Temporary hires helped fill the gap, while the Service tried to get more qualified men to enlist for a one-year period. The physical qualifying requirements were stiff, obviously including swimming. No mathematical or science knowledge was required. At the time, "spoilsman" (inexperienced men) were employed until such time as they could be replaced. The key requirement was to pass the physical examination performed by a doctor.

The 1906 Annual Report listed the number of lives saved by the nation's life-saving stations and the method of rescue:

     218 persons saved by lifeboats
   1,026 persons saved by surfboats
     218 persons saved by power lifeboats
      22 persons saved by power launches
     213 persons saved by river life skiffs
     330 persons saved by breeches buoy
      62 persons saved by other station boats
     189 persons saved by other means

In addition, 1,245 vessels were aided or warned of danger by signals from surfmen and took evasive action thus preventing disaster.

During the 1907 congressional hearings, the following exchange took place:

> "Mr. WINTHROP. *Last year the surfboat was used 997 times in making over 1,300 trips. The self-righting and self-bailing lifeboats were used 57 times, making 75 trips. The power lifeboat was used 132 times, making 157 trips. The breeches buoy was used 12 times, making 212 trips; and the wreck gun was used 17 times, firing 37 shots.*
>
> *The* CHAIRMAN. *How many persons were brought ashore by the breeches buoy?*
>
> *Mr.* WINTHROP. *There were landed by the surfboats – shall I give all the different means? There were landed by the surfboats 1,147 persons; by the lifeboats, 89 persons; by the power lifeboats, 145 persons; by the power launches, 176 persons; by the river life skiffs, 83 persons; by the breeches buoy, 198 persons; and by other station boats, 518 persons. There were also rescued 73 persons –*
>
> *The* CHAIRMAN. *What is the grand total of all those rescues?*
>
> *Mr.* WINTHROP. *The grand total is 2,429 lives."*

The single individual who played the most important role and who reorganized and managed the U.S. Life-Saving Service was *Sumner Increase Kimball*, a Treasury Department chief clerk who was first appointed in 1871 as Chief of the Revenue Marine Bureau. In 1878 he was appointed General Superintendent of the U.S. Life-Saving Service and he transformed the previous mismanaged volunteer service force into an organized professional government operated entity. *Kimball's* tenure lasted throughout the entire existence of the service and spanned 37 years. *Kimball* established all of the Life-Saving Stations on the nation's three coasts and the Great Lakes. His innovations of techniques, selection of new life-saving equipment, implementation of regulations and training greatly improved the service.

Sumner Increase Kimball

It is estimated the Service saved 177,000 lives during the period from 1878 to 1915 (37 years) prior to its merger with the U.S. Revenue Cutter Service (the predecessor of the U.S. Coast Guard).

Development and Improvement of Life-Saving Equipment

There were two fundamental purposes of the Life-Saving Service. The first, as its name implies is to save lives when a shipwreck occurred. As the service grew, a varied assortment of life-saving equipment evolved and through its years the equipment and "tools of the trade" were improved to include a variety of designs of surf boats, breeches buoys, guns that fired life lines to ships and communications equipment.

The second purpose of the Life-Saving Service was to prevent the grounding and foundering on rocks, reef and shores. Each station patrolled a beachfront. Surfmen watched from the station's lookout tower during the day and patrolled segments of beaches at night on the lookout for any vessel that appeared headed for danger. The beach patrol surfman was equipped with signaling devices to warn ships that were standing in danger that they needed to change course.

The effectiveness of the crew of the life-saving station in great part depended upon the mutual understanding of the stranded vessel's own crew and the procedures used by the life-saving station crew. Great efforts were made to distribute information to ship masters and ship owners on how the shore station life-saving crewmembers operated when sighting a vessel in distress. Information was made available in ports and customhouses to be distributed to vessels to better acquaint shipmasters with procedures.

> *"Each patrolman carries "Coston" signals. Upon discovering a vessel standing in danger, he ignites one of them which emits a bright red flame of about 2 minutes duration to warn off or if the vessel be ashore, to let the crew know that they are discovered and assistance is at hand.*
>
> *If the vessel is not discovered by the patrol immediately after striking, rockets or flare-up lights should be burned, or, if the weather be foggy, guns should be fired to attract attention as the patrolman may be some distance away on the other part of his beat.*

Masters are particularly cautioned, if they should be driven ashore any way in the neighborhood of the stations, especially on any sandy coasts where there is not much danger of the vessel breaking up immediately, to remain on board until assistance arrives and under no circumstances should they attempt to land through the surf in their own boats until the last hope of assistance from shore has vanished. Often when comparatively smooth at sea a dangerous surf is running, which is not perceptible four hundred yards off shore, and the surf when viewed from the vessel never appears so dangerous as it is. Many lives have unnecessarily been lost by crews of stranded vessels being thus deceived and attempting to land in the ship's boats.

The difficulties of rescue by operations from shore are greatly increased where anchors are let go after entering the breakers as frequently done, and chances of life correspondingly lessened.

The Life-Saving Station crew proceeds to the wreck by water or the lighter surfboat is hauled overland to a point opposite the wreck and launched, as circumstances allow.

Upon reaching your vessel, the directions and orders of the keeper (who always commands and steers the boat) should be implicitly obeyed. Any headlong rush and crowding should be prevented and the captain of the vessel should remain on board to preserve order until every person has left. Women, children and helpless persons shall be passed into the boat first. Goods or baggage will positively not be taken into the boat until all persons are landed. If any be passed in against the keeper's recommendation, he is fully authorized to throw the same overboard.

Should it be inexpedient to use either the life boat or surfboat, recourse will be to use the wreck gun and beech apparatus for the rescue by breeches buoy or the life car.

A shot with a small line attached will be fired across your vessel. Get hold of the line as soon as possible and haul on board until to get the tail block with a whip or endless line rove through it. This tailblock should be hauled on board as quickly as possible to prevent the whip drifting off with the set and fouling with the wreckage. Therefore if you have been driven into the rigging where but one or two men can work to advantage, cut the shot line and run it through some available block, such as the throat or peak halyard's block or any block which will afford a fair lead or even between the ratline that as many as possible may assist in hauling.

Attached to the tail block will be a tally board with the following directions in English on one side and French on the other. Make the tail of the block fast to the lower mast well up. If the masts are gone, then to the best place you can find. Cast off the shot line, see that the rope in the block runs free and show a signal to the shore."

With the inception of the Life-Saving Service and during its life span, life-saving apparatus, or "appliances" as they were called, were developed and improved. Every year a distinguished board of experts would convene and evaluate proposals and/or test new equipment, ideas and patents. As each year passed, improved equipment was purchased and added to station inventories.

2 The Service

The most serious obstacle that surfmen faced was transporting heavy life-saving equipment along the sandy beaches to where a vessel was stranded or in peril. At times, the heavy surfboat could not be launched at the station. It was sometimes transported on a four-wheel cart, pulled by the crew or by a horse team over the beach to get near the wreck site.

Each station was provided with the government list of equipment including:

> "One 5-inch "eprouvette" mortar, weighing with its bed and three (3) balls about 350 pounds.
> One shot-line together with a faking box in which it is carried 80 pounds.
> One set of 2½ inch hauling lines, 250 fathoms in length with blocks weighing 300 pounds
> One 4-½ inch hawser weighing 600 pounds
> A breeches buoy crotch and sand anchor weighing 125 pounds
> One 'Life Car' weighing about 225 pounds or breeches buoy and related equipment."

The breeches buoy apparatus itself was much lighter, weighing only 21 pounds. It required lighter cordage and saved considerable weight in instances where a small number of people were to be rescued and they had no injuries; or when no small children, aged persons or invalids were involved. Being lightweight, it could also be summoned to the scene by adjacent stations.

All of this equipment had to be dragged by seven men from the life-saving station to the location of the disaster, and almost always in weather that was serious enough to cause the disaster, be it gales, rain, snow or ice. The surfmen had little or no volunteer help since populated settlements were few if any along the remote beaches. By the time surfmen reached the disaster scene they were often exhausted from the trek and the burdens of hauling 1,700 pounds of appliances over wet sand or mud. Setting up equipment required extra effort in raising voices to be heard over the howling wind and pounding surf. The difficulty of the labor added greatly to limiting their endurance for the actual rescue operations.

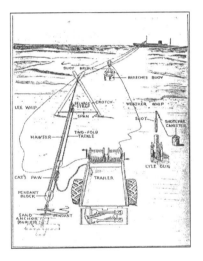

The beach apparatus was comprised of a number of components that were all transported over the beach in a cart pulled by the harnessed station crew.
Sketch LSS Annual Report
Photo U.S. Coast Guard Files

As the service matured it recognized that "draught animals" (horses) could be used to pull these heavy loads. An urgent appropriation was made in 1879 as a result of acknowledging that loads up to 1,000 lbs were borne by seven surfmen harnessed to a loaded cart. Over wet sand

and leaning into a winter gale, men were exhausted and fatigued by the time they had reached the disaster scene. Their slow plodding progress added delays in reaching the wreck and in many cases delays meant life or death to the crew of a disabled vessel. A single horse was placed at several stations during the winter months. The horses could be readily obtained for only the cost of feed and shelter and they improved the efficiency and stamina of the surfmen during a rescue.

Surfboats

The heavy surfboat was the other back up. It required the entire crew to launch it and then row through surf. In many cases it was impossible to use if surf and seas were high. The surfboat underwent modification after modification to mature along with the Service. With training, surfmen learned what it could bear and do. Proficiency was achieved through drill and discipline and efficiency reached its height. The surfboat became endeared. To the surfmen there was "nothing floating to compare with it in the world".

Retrieval of the surfboat was also an arduous effort. As soon as the boat touched bottom, the crew shipped oars, jumped into the water to prevent it from broaching and began a grueling effort to haul the heavy surfboat up onto the beach. Stations with horses re-launched the four-wheel cradle cart and used a horse team to retrieve the surfboat.

There were many improvements to the surfboat and lifeboat when the U.S. Coast Guard inherited the Service. The surfboat was considered light enough to be launched from the beach or carried by cart to the wreck site. Lifeboats generally were heavier requiring launching ways or rails. The standard lifeboat became a 36-ft powered vessel with a beam of 9 ft, having five thwarts and a 35-horsepower motor. The design was self-righting and self-bailing thereby providing much needed security to the crew. Beebe McLellan introduced other boats of 28 to 32 feet, both with and without power and all with self-bailing and righting qualities. These lighter boats replaced the older surfboats that used auxiliary sails in addition to rowing thwarts.

Line throwing guns

The process of firing a line to a stranded vessel was examined and improved throughout the life of the Service. The line was attached to a projectile. The series of models, modifications and developments of both guns and projectiles revealed a constant change of apparatus and methods. The basic concept was to shoot a light line to the stranded vessel, pull a heavier line on board and rig the "breeches buoy", a life preserver buoy fitted with canvas pants (breeches) that the rescued person rode back to shore. The process was complicated and life station crews practiced constantly.

A reenactment of preparing the Lyle gun for firing
Photo courtesy of H&S

2 The Service

There were strict regulations and specifications outlined for the equipment to be used. In 1878 the recommended gun was specified as "the caliber of the gun will depend on the size of the line used and the range required".

> "For ranges of 300 yards or less with heavy line a 3 inch gun should be used. For ranges of 400 yards or less with a braided line a 2.5 inch bronze gun should be used. For ranges of 200 yards or less a 2 in. gun should be sufficient."

Captain *David A. Lyle* of the U.S. Army became famous for developing the surf gun (cannon) and throughout the years of the Life-Saving Service he served as the chief advisor to the Apparatus Committee. In 1877, while still a lieutenant, he devised a gun and shot that weighed only 202 pounds and attained a maximum range of 695 yards (a third of a mile). This gun was selected to be supplied to all Life-Saving Stations as soon as possible.

METHOD OF USING THE LIFE SAVING APPARATUS

The gun was only as effective as the ability of the attached line to cleanly leave the wooden box where it had been "faked" down. In some cases due to wind, poor marksmanship or the stranded vessel's crew inability to secure the line, the gun had to be reloaded, the line retrieved, re-faked into the box and fired again. Faking the line or preparing the line to fire without tangling was a process that was repeatedly practiced. A good faker could load a faking box of 600 yards of line in 25 to 28 minutes. A "clumsy" man would take 40 to 50 minutes. Three men were used to fake the line into the box. The "faker" placed the line carefully aligned with the pins in the box, another man fed the line to the faker, and the third played the line off the supply reel.

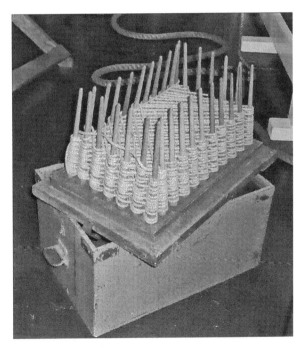

Faking rack: After the line was faked, the wood pins were removed before firing
Photo U.S. Coast Guard Museum, by author

2 The Service

Beach Patrol

A lookout was posted in the watchtower of the station building during the daytime hours. They were not allowed to sit, and had to stand on their feet during their 4-hour shift. From the height of the watchtower the lookout had a 180-degree view of the horizon out to five miles or more. At night, regardless of the weather, the beach patrol of normally two surfmen walking in opposite directions was activated and the surfmen were required to trudge along the soft sand and rocks on the look out for vessels standing in danger or in distress. Visibility of a beach patrol surfman on a clear night was limited by the curvature of the earth. The horizon was less than three miles away and a ship which was "hull down" (below the horizon) was visible only by the height of its mast and sails above the horizon. The daytime tower watch under clear weather conditions could see upwards of 6-7 miles dependant on the height of the lookout perch. The danger came when a vessel ventured into shallow water closer to the beach.

Both the tower watch and beach patrol were boring duties. The beach patrol was burdened with signal flares, a watchman clock, boots, rain gear and winter clothing; so it was not only boring but tedious trudging. Those discomforts were coupled with working outdoors in gale force winds and driving rain. These adverse conditions created the most likely time for a vessel to be in danger and required extra alertness. With these physical challenges and the low pay, much stress was added to the surfman's job.

With stations spaced five to seven miles apart, the beach patrol usually required a walk of two to three miles on either side of the life-saving station, hopefully meeting the patrolman from the adjacent station. Patrols exchanged medallion "checks" with their station numbers on them and then turn back and patrolled the distance back to their station. The surfman would then continue his patrol in the opposite direction toward the next adjacent station and repeat the procedure. Where an adjacent station could not be built such as Brenton Reef, a key was posted that fit into a clock mechanism carried by the patrol surfman to verify he had made his rounds. The Service implied that this procedure was to protect the surfman from "unjust negligence" charges of not completing his patrol, but it was well known it served to prove to the keeper that each man completed his patrol.

Excerpt from Narragansett Pier Station log indicating beach patrol assignments on December 27, 1908:

2 The Service

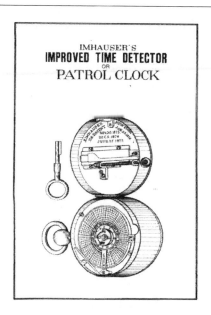

Various clocks were tested by beach patrol surfmen to validate that the patrol was completing his nightly watch. Many questioned reliability and various configurations were tried. For example, the Sandy Point Life-Saving Station on Block Island tested a Beyer Patrol Watchman Portable Clock. It was to be punched every 7½ minutes in the station and at a key post outside on the beach. It failed to record after six weeks of testing.

One improved model is described below:

> "Imhauser's improved time-detector or patrol clock - This watchman's clock is to be carried by surfmen at remote stations where patrol checks cannot be used to advantage. It is designed to protect the surfmen against unjust charges of neglecting their patrol. It also furnishes the Department with documentary evidence with which to refute such charges against the patrolmen. Unless tampered with it gives indisputable evidence of their whereabouts during the

hours of patrol. The paper dial is perforated by the insertion of a metal key at each of the patrol key posts and forms a record which is filed for future reference."

Not all beach patrol equipment was satisfactory. The Service relentlessly pursued new developments and whenever possible tested them at various stations to deem their suitability. For example in 1902, a new kerosene-fueled hand lantern called the Brundy Lantern was offered to the evaluation board. The new lantern looked to be very promising as an improvement to the current hand lantern carried by the beach patrols. Six stations, two on the Great Lakes, two in Massachusetts and two in Rhode Island (Narragansett Pier and Point Judith) were selected to test the device. The lantern was found to burn brighter and at one wreck site, it was the only one that worked. It failed, however to burn for more than four hours and its weight was twice that of the lanterns currently in use. The consensus from all six stations was that it was unsatisfactory for all around use.

In 1898, in their endeavor to find a better buoyant life preserver than one filled with cork, a series of tests were undertaken with preservers filled with reindeer hair, which reportedly was much more buoyant. The following year's annual report carried no further mention of the rejection or acceptance of this idea.

Inspections

While experienced keepers were selected and assigned to station as both the leader and trainer, it was only through actual site inspections that the Service could confirm and measure the competency of the station and crew. The role was assigned to Assistant Inspectors of the U.S. Revenue Marine Service.

Each station was visited once each year and as early in the winter as possible to get any deficiencies corrected and station crews organized. The stations of Long Island, New York and Rhode Island were difficult to reach since most were situated at remote locations and presented difficult access because of undergrowth and seldom traveled roads. Point Judith Station in 1877 is an example where, other than random farmhouses, no civilization existed within ten miles.

A *New York Times* correspondent accompanied three inspectors (including a doctor) from the Marine Hospital Service to Point Judith Station and relates the following:

> *We passed neighboring farmers who raked seaweed up to the beach to decay for manure emitting a sickening smell that floats for miles into the interior giving the whole of that part of the little state the odor of an apothecary's storeroom.*
>
> *Arriving at the station at supper time, several of the crew members are absent, being allowed to eat at home. A crew member rushes upstairs and in minutes the flag staff is covered with flags including a pennant and under it a red and blue flag, being the signal for assembling the of all the men. Shortly all the crew and the keeper arrived and the inspection began.*
>
> *The crew's first duty is to save lives. For this purpose they are lined up and instructed in the method of reviving apparently drowned persons. The inspector who is a doctor*

selects the most intelligent looking crewmember and asks "What do you do if you find a apparently drowned person on the beach?"

"First lay him in a dry place and if there is any danger of him freezing to death bring him at once to the station. Clean out the sand from his mouth and lay him face down. I should make a pillow either with a log heap of sand or my coat and put it under his stomach, then press hard on the small of his back so the water would be out of him. I should then lay him on his back and press on his ribs stomach to produce artificial breathing. If this failed after a half hour, I should get the medicine cabinet and give him some snuff."

Every station is provided with two bottles of brandy, two of sherry, a bottle of snuff, one ammonia and preparation of iron to be used as a styptic for wounds.

Although the station looked clean, it did not satisfy the inspectors and the keeper was intellectually drubbed. The crew was called down one at a time and to be questioned on other matters. It was evident the crew would make better work getting a boat out through the surf than answering puzzling questions.

The men then were ordered out to exercise the beach apparatus and equipment comprising the surfboat, lines, hawsers and mortar for shooting the breeches buoy line over a stricken vessel."

Inspection also included reviewing authorized equipment lists and personnel bunks and uniforms, the efficiency of the apparatus and discipline of the men.

Communications

It did not take long to recognize that a means of communication was necessary between the life-saving crews and the vessel in distress. The first communications between shore and ship was by "speaking trumpets", but in short time visual signals were used. Flags, flares, lanterns and rockets were put to use. What was missing was the interpretation or understanding of the signals and responses.

Flag signals (vexillology) had always been part of communications at sea. Vessels exchanged information as they were hailed, but there was no protocol among the users. A Code of Signals emerged for the merchant service devised by Captain *Frederick Marryat* of the British Royal Navy in 1817 as a stepping stone to the International Code of Signals published by the British Board of Trade in 1855. Seventy thousand messages could be sent or received with these flags and combinations thereof. In 1887 the Chief Signal Officer of the U.S. Army, in cooperation with the Life-Saving Service, developed a simple code of Danger and Distress signals for use between ships and shore stations and included them in the appendix of the *International Code of Signals for Merchant Vessels*. For example, the international signal "JD" was adopted for signifying "you are standing into danger". Flag staffs were constructed at all Life-Saving Service stations for daytime use. The Collector of Customs at each port passed copies of the signals to incoming and departing shipmasters. Today, almost the identical signals are included as a chapter in the International Signal Book. The ship to shore and the shore to ship signals consist of manual signals, flags and lights. The lights are red, green or white flares, colored star rockets, or orange smoke. All have distinctive meanings allowing the ship's crew and shore crews to understand each other's intentions.

As telephone technology advanced, all district life-saving stations were connected within their districts to other stations and their district superintendent's office. Stations were able to readily communicate with each other, thereby requesting assistance of a nearby station, either for more surfmen, extra surfboats or beach apparatus.

Formation of Districts

Rhode Island stations were first assigned in the Third District, along with a number of Long Island, New York stations. In June 1900 an act of Congress realigned the stations and placed all the Rhode Island stations and only a single New York station on Fishers Island under jurisdiction of the Third District. All of the other stations, were designated upward one level; e.g., the remainder of the Third District went to the Fourth District, and those in the Fourth went to Fifth, etc.

The formality of the Service evolved as new stations were established and additional reporting requirements were put in place. Part of this change was due to the need to keep accurate records, and another reason was to document disaster incidents in order to justify congressional appropriations necessary to maintain the stations and life-saving crews. The record keeping requirements were exacting and each station had to document any activity from significant shipwrecks and strandings to providing assistance to vessels dragging anchors. Even minor incidents, such as providing shelter overnight to a weary sailor who was cold or rowing out to a vessel to unload a pilot who had no means of getting ashore, were required to be reported. Of course, loss of life and the saving of lives were paramount and when combined, became the most significant statistic in the justification of the existence of stations. During the period between 1875 and 1904, the average number of lives lost by shipwreck disasters numbered 250-300 each year. In 1903 1,281 lives were lost.

All life-saving attempts were not successful and rowing into the surf in an attempt to save a life sometimes turned into another disaster. On March 17, 1902 seven surfmen from the Monomoy Life-Saving Station on the southern fringe of Cape Cod attempted a rescue of five men off the stranded coal barge *Wadena*. All twelve men drowned after the crew of the *Wadena* was taken off the barge and into the surfboat. Panic ensued, capsizing the surfboat and throwing the Life-Saving Service crew and the barge crew into the raging sea.

As the number of incidents increased the Light-Saving Service categorized them into four major groups:

1. *Foundered*: vessels lost, sunk or disabled due leaking or capsizing
2. *Strandings*: vessels who went aground on beaches, rocks, reefs or shoals
3. *Collisions*: incidents between two or more vessels
4. *Other*: fire, irrespective of results; scuttling or any intentional damage to vessels; collisions with fields or quantities of ice, although vessels may be sunk thereby; striking on sunken wrecks, anchors, buoys, piers, or bridges; leakage (except when vessel

foundered or went ashore for safety); loss of masts, sails, boats, or any portion of a vessel's equipment; capsizing, when vessels did not sink; damage to machinery; fouling of anchors; striking of lightning; explosion of boilers; breakage of wheels; also water-logged, missing, and abandoned vessels

The cataloging also included the identification by vessel types. Sailing vessels included were schooners, barks, barkentines, brigs, and ships (full rigged). Engine-fitted vessels were either steamers or steamships. In 1879 schooners outnumbered all other vessels by a ratio of 3:1. By 1906 coastal sailing packets were rapidly being forced out of business as steam and other fossil fuel powered vessels replaced them.

Excerpt from 1879 Annual LSS Report:

TABLE 7.—*Abstract of returns of disasters to vessels on the* ATLANTIC *and* GULF *coasts during the year ending June 30, 1879, showing the number of vessels and distinguishing their* DESCRIPTION.

Description of vessels.	July.	August.	September.	October.	November.	December.	January.	February.	March.	April.	May.	June.	Total.
Barges		1		3				2	1	1			9
Barks	2	2	3	2	3	2	7	5	5	1	1	2	34
Barkentines							1			1			2
Brigs	1		4	3	4	1	3	1	4	5	1	2	29
Brigantines						1	1						3
Canal-boats			1						1				2
Ferry-boats	1		3	2		2	2	1	1	2			13
Schooners	39	34	42	150	62	60	45	31	69	59	33	32	656
Scows	1						1						7
Ships				1	1		1		2	1			7
Sloops	4	3	1	10		1	4	2	1	4	3		34
Steamers	6	6	11	22	4	8	7	8	7	9	8	13	109
Steamships	3	4		3	2	3	5	2		1	2	5	30
Unknown	1		2		1	1							5
Total	58	50	66	196	77	81	76	53	92	80	50	57	936

Another benchmark used by the Service to highlight the number of tragedies was to list the causes of the shipwrecks.

2 The Service

One selective compilation states:

Cause	Number of Wrecks
Weather	420
Navigation errors	42
Equipment and machinery failures	22
Other	127

(fire, ice, leaks, struck rock, no pilot, defective tow line, etc.)

Rhode Island Shipwreck Archives

A variety of sources through the centuries of Rhode Island's maritime history have accumulated and archived the records of marine disasters and shipwrecks. Commonly, the need was to identify sunken vessels lying just below the water in order to warn navigators of the hazard. Navigation charts were periodically updated to show the position and depth of these hazards. New wrecks were reported in the *Notice to Mariners* until such time as they were noted on navigation charts. Historians over the years had noted significant incidents as they related to local communities in terms of loss of life and economic impact. The interests of other groups were more recreational, such as underwater diving clubs and organizations that saw excitement in exploring wrecks and perhaps even finding valuable artifacts. Along with them, were the fishing enthusiasts who had always known wrecks attract schools of fish. The popularity of both old and newly found underwater wrecks soared with the advent of scuba equipment and the ability to explore at depth.

As a result, databases, special charts, books and magazine articles identifying wrecks in Narragansett Bay, Block Island Sound and Rhode Island Sound became available. These sources exist in multiple forms. The State of Rhode Island possesses the most comprehensive and reliable database archived by the Historic Preservation and Heritage Commission. It has a listing over 1,000 shipwrecks. The Rhode Island Ocean Special Management Program (Ocean SAMP), under the direction of the Coastal Resource Management Council (CMRC) and the University of Rhode Island (URI), serves as the primary management and regulatory group. They have identified other sources including the Rhode Island Marine Archaeology Project (RIMAP), the National Oceanographic and Atmospheric Administration Office (NOAA), Office of Coast Surveys, Automatic Wreck and Obstruction Information System (AWOIS) and the Northern Shipwrecks Data Base which lists 1,200 Rhode Island wrecks. URI maintains three different datasets that include a working archaeological database that contains 618 shipwrecks in Rhode Island waters and an historical database from sources such as historic charts, U.S. Coast Guard and Navy records.

Other sources that augment the databases include dive guidebooks such as the *Rhode Island Adventure Diving II* and *The Bell Tolls: Shipwrecks & Lighthouses, Volume 1, Block Island*.

More recently the Beavertail Lighthouse Museum Association under the direction of their marine historian *James Jenney* has been documenting not only wrecks, but also marine disasters. The collection includes detailed vessel, cargo and owner information, plus visual chart location data. *Jenney* estimates that over 2,000 identified incidents including shipwrecks have taken place and he continues to research and document their related details.

The SAMP study focuses on the waters around Block Island where, over three centuries, heavy levels of commercial traffic experienced storms, strong currents, and dense fog. These factors and the lack of navigational aids also resulted in collisions. The other high concentration of shipwrecks was along the southern shore of Rhode Island, the corridor that runs from Watch Hill to Point Judith. Incidents are common in this area because of very high levels of both passenger and commercial shipping transiting to and from New England ports. The late 1800s saw dramatic increases in shipping, particularly cargos of coal to fuel the Industrial Revolution. Coal schooners and barges transported coal from the Appalachian Mountains through mid-Atlantic ports from Virginia north to the New England states.

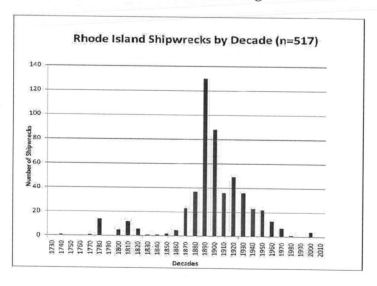

SAMP shipwreck distribution in Rhode Island waters from 1730 to 2010

Life Station Building Designs

The buildings that housed the Life-Saving Station crews and their equipment were also improved and somewhat standardized. Some of the structures were classical gothic and in a form of beautiful architecture rarely seen today. The Life-Saving Stations attempted to standardize wherever possible. As a result a commonality developed from 1848 to 1929 and stations were often identifiable by their architectural designs. Rhode Island saw six different configurations over the years:

Deal type	1882-1885	Brenton Point Station
Quonnie type	1891-1908	Quonochontaug Station
		Sandy Point Station
Port Huron type	1898-1908	Watch Hill Station
Bibb type	1882-1888	Point Judith Station
		New Shoreham
Isle of Shoals type	1910-1912	Green Hill Station
Red House type	1870-1880	Block Island Station
One of a kind		Narragansett Pier Station

Interestingly, the Rhode Island Quonochontaug Station was built in 1898 and replicated at 20 different locations along the Atlantic Coast and Lake Michigan between 1898 and 1908. Identified simply as a "Quonnie" type because Quonochontaug was such a tongue twister, difficult to pronounce even by Rhode Islanders.

In Rhode Island only three of the nine stations that stretched across the southern shore and Block Island are still standing. One on Block Island has been transformed into a private home and is not recognizable as a life-saving station. The Narragansett Pier Station is now a restaurant (see Chapter

4), and the Brenton Point Station was rebuilt as the Castle Hill U.S. Coast Guard Station and remains active.

1898 Spanish America War

Little has been written about the coastal stations when war broke out with Spain in 1898. The government immediately realized the need for a line of signal stations along both the Atlantic and Gulf Coasts to provide early warning if enemy vessels should appear and to transmit available information to Naval authorities in Washington, D.C. With little hesitation it was realized that the existing Life-Saving Stations could be adapted to fill this role. Life-saving crews were well trained in visual signal communications. They were already trained to watch seaward both day and night, accustomed to patrolling beaches, well disciplined and use to 24 hours a day operations. Only extending their operation schedules into their inactive months of June and July was required. Plus, the stations were located at frequent intervals and at important points.

It was General Superintendent *Sumner Increase Kimball* who immediately suggested the use of his coastal stations because simple basic orders could be transmitted to stations within hours. Moreover, since the stations were in close proximity to each other and could quickly communicate by means of telephone, information could be relayed directly to the office of the superintendent or to the Coastal Signal Service in Washington. *Kimball's* offer was immediately accepted and three-fourths of all the life-saving stations on the Atlantic and Gulf Coasts were commissioned as Coast Signal Stations. The system was further expanded to include lighthouse stations and Weather Bureau Stations. When completed, the coastal warning communications system had 233 stations, 139 of which were Life-Saving Stations.

The swiftness of the transition to this dual role of Life-Saving Stations resulted in the impossibility of the enemy to threaten the coast. The importance was noted by the naval staff, "They effectively served every purpose of their establishment and on occasion rewarded rendering service in instances of extreme importance by advising movement of government vessels."

Interestingly at that time, the U.S. Government was overjoyed that military type outposts or "pickets" as they called them could be called upon to prepare the country for any future emergency and the cost for maintaining them as a military establishments during peace time was at no additional expense.

By 1900 the fame of the U.S. Life-Saving Stations was recognized around the world, even though the total number of vessel casualties were decreasing. In contrast, the value of lost property of both vessels and cargo had increased in the United States and other countries. In January 1899 a letter addressed to the General Superintendent was received from the Commander of the Imperial Japanese Navy, *Count Kozo Yoshii,* requesting data relating to the life-saving beach apparatus used by the United States. At that time the Japanese had established the Imperial Japanese Society for Life-Saving comprised of twelve stations. Between 1898 and 1890 they had saved 1,651 persons and over 300 ships.

The request by *Yoshii* was brought before the U.S. Congress. On the recommendation of the General Superintendent and the Secretary of the Treasury authorization was given to provide the Japanese with a complete set of beach apparatus including a Lyle gun, other appliances and an apparatus cart for their transportation. This gift was duly recorded in Japanese periodicals and newspapers as an "affair of utmost cordiality from the United States".

Chapter 3

The Rhode Island Stations

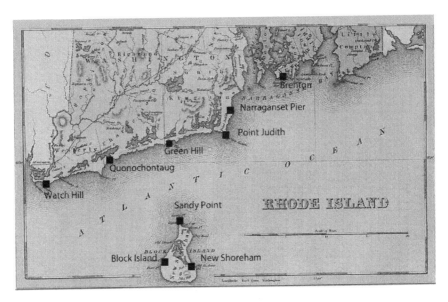

From the early 17th century colonial period, shipwrecks were not uncommon in Rhode Island's waters. Three hundred fifty miles of coastline consisting of rocks and sandy beaches, coupled with uncharted underwater hazards, currents and unreliable or nonexistent navigation aids, contributed to a vast accumulation of shipwrecks along its shores.

The largest percentage of shipwrecks occurred along the State's southernmost shore that fronts the Atlantic Ocean. Rhode Island and Block Island Sounds and the waters around Block Island itself define this region. The area is mostly a flat moraine of barrier beaches with scattered reefs and rocks. Estimates from the period of 1650 to present day

3 The Rhode Island Stations

exceed 2,000 known underwater wrecks and marine disasters. Loss of cargo and life over those years has not been calculated since there are no accurate data for strandings or events where there were not losses of vessels. Six hundred seventy five vessels were assisted along the shores of Rhode Island in 1895 alone according the District Superintendent's report. It should be noted that men serving in the U.S. Light House Service also aided in incidents of vessels sinking or being stranded.

An early effort in Rhode Island to help the offshore mariner was the establishment of seaward looking lighthouses. Beavertail Light in 1749, Watch Hill Light in 1808, Point Judith Light in 1809 and Block Island Light (Sandy Point) in 1829. As coastal shipping comprised of sailing packets and schooners moved more and more cargo, passenger vessels also began populating the seaways. It was after the first passenger steamboat named the *Ugly* appeared on Narragansett Bay in 1817 that the clamor for more navigation aids resulted in the establishment of 26 additional lighthouses, including two lightships. These efforts to prevent loss of lives from ship disasters set into motion specialized dedicated services as national laws were enacted.

When life-saving became a national law in 1848, the Watch Hill, Rhode Island station (1850) became one of the first to be established. It was supplied with a metal lifeboat, rockets, mortars, lanterns, shovels, ropes and fundamental supplies. For over 20 years the U.S. government provided equipment and facilities to Watch Hill while the local community was required to supply the volunteer manpower to save lives. It took time and more disasters for the government to cede to pressures of those concerned and to organize the more formal organization, the U.S. Life-Saving Service.

Watch Hill is the western door of Rhode Island's maritime avenue. The long stretch of Long Island Sound is generally protected all the way from New York City and the Connecticut ports of Stanford, Bridgeport, New Haven, Saybrook, New London and Mystic. These cities were all involved in maritime commerce. Vessels from those locations plying the ports of New England passed Watch Hill, as did ships from northern New England ports sailing in the opposite direction. The narrow and treacherous strait know as the Race, because of its fast current at the western end of Long Island Sound, shot transiting vessels by Watch Hill; and its various underwater rock formations and reefs were hazards awaiting many shipwrecks.

The Stations

Soon after the formal organization of the U.S. Life-Saving Service teams of investigators were formed and directed to visit every life-saving station to evaluate both the condition of each facility and the quality and qualifications of the surfmen. The 1877 report for the Third District (including the Rhode Island stations) was not complementary.

"The stations were generally neat and orderly, but at a few there was the lack of proper discipline and in some cases the keepers were not alive to the important nature of their charge. The main fault observed in these instances was the loose and unsystematic manner in which they permitted their crews to perform the duty of patrolling the beach

between stations during the night, evading as far as possible the strict attention of the regulation in reference to this cardinal feature of the service. It was found that one or two of the keepers absented themselves much of the time from the stations leaving them in charge of some member of the crew. These delinquencies caused three Keepers to be recommended for dismissal and other persons appointed in their places. The surfmen were generally qualified and it was only necessary to remove four of them."

Thirty-five keepers and 200 surfmen were evaluated. Four keepers were allowed to resign because of their age, impaired energy and their faithful service. They left with a distinction recorded in their jackets as "without blemish". 1877 was also a disastrous shipwreck year for Third District stations. There were 12 major calamities where 28 people lost their lives.

U.S. Life-Saving Station Locations in Rhode Island

1896 listing of Rhode Island stations

THIRD DISTRICT.

COASTS OF RHODE ISLAND AND LONG ISLAND.

Name of station.	State.	Locality.	Approximate position. Latitude, north.	Longitude, west.
Brentons Point	R. I.	On Prices Neck	41 26 58	71 20 10
Narragansett Pier	R. I.	Northern part of the town	41 25 45	71 27 20
Point Judith	R. I.	Near light	41 21 40	71 29 00
Quonochontaug	R. I.	7½ miles east of Watch Hill light.	41 19 50	71 43 10
Watch Hill	R. I.	Near light	41 18 20	71 51 30
New Shoreham	R. I.	Block Island, east side, near landing	41 10 20	71 33 30
Block Island	R. I.	Block Island, west side, near Dickens Point	41 09 40	71 36 40

(The Green Hill and Block Island Sandy Point Stations were added after 1896.)

From 1872 to 1938 a total of nine stations were constructed and operated in Rhode Island by the U.S. Life-Saving Service. For administrative purposes the first four Rhode Island Stations (Narragansett Pier, Point Judith, Block Island NE and Block Island SW), established in 1876, were placed under the jurisdiction of the Service's Third District, along with thirty-three Long Island stations headquartered in Bridgehampton, New York. At the height of the Service's operations in 1892 a total of thirty-nine stations of the Third District stretched along the coastline from Newport, RI to New York City.

In 1908 a redistricting took place. Eight Rhode Island stations and a station on Fishers Island, New York were regrouped as the only stations in Third District. The Fishers Island Station was on a narrow 5½-mile island, straddling the dangerous west entrance to Long Island Sound. It was located on the west shore of East Harbor, about four miles southwest of Watch Hill Station. Because of its close proximity to Watch Hill it was included with the eight Rhode Island stations. Green Hill Station was added in 1912, completing the nine Rhode Island stations. With the addition of the Green Hill the Third District had a total of ten stations stretching from Brenton Point (Price's Neck), Rhode Island to Fishers Island, New York.

Each Rhode Island station was manned by six surfmen from July 1 through May 31. The heaviest and most frequent storms were experienced from March 31 to November 1, and an additional surfman was assigned during that time period.

Rhode Island Life-Saving Stations

Station	Established	Status
Block Island		
Block Island (Salt Pond)	1872	active*
New Shoreham Station	1874	discontinued 1947
Sandy Point Station	1898	discontinued 1922
Watch Hill Station	1879	active*
Brenton Point		
Price's Neck Station	1884	destroyed 1938
moved to Castle Hill	1939	active*
Point Judith Station	1876	active*
Narragansett Pier Station	1872	discontinued 1937
Quonochontaug Station	1891	destroyed 1938
Green Hill Station	1912	destroyed 1938

*currently operated by the U.S. Coast Guard

Three of the stations, Block Island, Point Judith and Brenton Point (Castle Hill), continue to be operated by the present day U.S. Coast Guard. Remarkably, two of the old reconstructed life-saving buildings are still in use by the Coast Guard (Block Island (Salt Pond) and Castle Hill. They are now Search and Rescue (SAR) units providing some of the basic services as their predecessors, in addition to the Homeland Security role of guarding our shores.

District Superintendent Herbert M. Knowles

From 1899, the Superintendent of the Third District was Captain *Herbert M. Knowles*. The Third District Assistant Superintendent, *Nichols Ball*, was stationed in New Shoreham (Block island), Rhode Island.

Capt. *Herbert M. Knowles* of Wakefield, RI served relentlessly as superintendent of the Third District for 38 years, starting out as a surfman for two years and then as keeper of the Point Judith Station for eleven years. He entered the service in 1876, succeeding his father at the Point Judith Station.

3 The Rhode Island Stations

Herbert M. Knowles

Knowles was born on March 26, 1856 on Point Judith near the lighthouse. He had been a surf fisherman, sailor, and wrecker. When the Life-Saving Station was established at Point Judith in 1876, he resigned a position as mate of a coastal schooner. He began his service with the Life-Saving Station on November 15 of that year as surfman No. 1 of the inaugural crew. His compensation was $40 per month ($1.33 per day).

In December 1878 *Knowles* was promoted to keeper of the Point Judith Life-Saving Station at a salary of $400 per year. He held that position until August 1899 when he was promoted to the position of Assistant District Superintendent (succeeding the late Capt. *John Waters*) at a salary of $1,000 per year. Later he was promoted to the position of District Superintendent at a salary of $1,600 per year.

In his 38 years of service in these various positions (which he earned by merit), he responded to more wrecks and had more rough experiences than any life-saver in the District, or perhaps on the Atlantic seaboard. In one year, he was responsible for saving more than 100 people from shipwrecks.

Knowles was appointed a member of the Board on Life-Saving Appliances in 1890 by the Secretary of the Treasury due to his special knowledge of boats and general workings of the Service. This board was later renamed the U.S. Life-Saving Devices Board and their responsibility was to evaluate and approve (or disapprove) various life-saving apparatus proposed for use at life-saving stations throughout the United States. *Knowles* submitted his letter of resignation to the U.S. Life-Saving Devices Board in October 1914.

Knowles was detailed to take charge of the national life-saving exhibit at the 1898 Trans Mississippi Exposition, held in Omaha, Nebraska. In this, like all other of his undertakings, he was a perfect success. He was the originator of the capsized lifeboat drill that became very popular, and of great interest at other expositions.

Around 1900, *Knowles* was further recognized for his valued services when he was appointed by the Secretary of the Treasury to a special committee of five to evaluate the feasibility of establishing mechanical power propulsion of surfboats and lifeboats.

In connection with his regular duties as a district officer, *Knowles* helped build the more than 70 miles of telephone line connecting the stations in his district. He personally kept the lines in repair as long as his official duties would permit, thus saving the Service the expense of a telephone lineman for over sixteen years.

The extreme exposure to the elements that *Knowles* experienced in the faithful discharge of various duties greatly impaired his hearing, and in a few years he became deaf. The low salary paid this efficient and dedicated officer, together with his resulting poor health and loss of hearing that occurred after serving the Service 31 years, earned him special recognition of Congress by placing him on waiting orders or permanent retirement.

Third District Reports

Annual reports of each Rhode Island Life-Saving Station, as were those of all several hundred other stations, were published in the annual *U.S. Life-Saving Service Report*. (Most of the events in subsequent chapters of this book are excerpts from those annual reports.) The reports include comprehensive details of events where loss of life was involved. It was required to report all incidents of strandings, use of the station lifeboat or breeches buoy equipment. In addition, the reports included warnings signaled to vessels in potential danger by the beach patrols. Logs and reports from each station were forwarded to District Superintendent *Knowles* in Wakefield who then consolidated the reports and sent them on to Washington DC.

3 The Rhode Island Stations

Excerpt from 1901 LSS Annual Report:

TABLE 66.— *List of places on the coasts of the United States where vessels have stranded during the last ten years—Continued.*

ATLANTIC AND GULF COASTS—Continued.

Name of place	1882	1883	1884	1885	1886	1887	1888	1889	1890	1891	Total
RHODE ISLAND—continued.											
Block Island—Continued.											
Northwest shore of	3	2				1					4
Sandy Point	1			1							2
South and southwest shore of	6	1	2	1		2			1		13
West side of	1	1				5	1		1		9
Charlestown Beach		1				1					2
Narragansett Bay:											
Beaver Tail Point	1		1								2
Black Point										1	1
Bonnet Point	1										1
Brentons Reef										1	1
Butter Ball Rock									1		1
Caseys Point					1						1
Castle Hill						2					2
Coddington Point									1		1
Conanicut Island		1			1				2		4
Despair Island				1							1
Dutch Island	1		2	1				1		2	7
Dyers Island (rocks off)					1		1				2
Fullers Rock, Providence River										1	1
Gould Island, Sakonnet River							1	1			2
Hog Island							1				1
Hope Island	1										1
Narragansett Pier	1		1		1		2		1		5
Nayat Point										1	1
Newport	2	1					1		4		8
Newtons Rock	1										1
Popasquash Point						1				1	2
Plum Beach Shoal	1				1		1				3
Prudence Island			2		1					2	5
Rose Island	1		1					1			3
Rumstick Shoal	1										1
Sakonnet Point			1		1	2				1	5
Warrens Point, Elishas Ledge							1				1
Warwick Neck		1		1	1						2
Wesqueague Beach											1
Wickford		1									1
Narragansett Bay, Little:											
Seal Rocks				1							1
Point Judith											
Eleven miles west of	1	1	3		2	2	2	3	1		15
Three miles northwest of								1			1
Squid Ledge		1					1		1		2
Quonocontaug Beach											3
Watch Hill	1				1	1		3		1	9
Catumb Reef				2	1					2	4
Napatree Point	2					2	1	1	2	4	14
Sugar Reef		1	1						1		3

All incidents were summarized in various forms and on occasion tabulations were carried from year to year. Table #66 from the 1891 Annual Report (see above) is an example of a compilation of vessels that stranded on Rhode Island shoals and rocks over a ten-year period. Note that the listings cover only stranding of vessels and not vessel losses that were tabulated separately. The Service did not record information on losses of cargo. While no Life-Saving Stations were located within Narragansett Bay and up to Providence, local harbor masters, pilots and revenue agents reported strandings within the Bay.

In 1908 District Commissioner *Knowles* testified to a Congressional committee and summarized the status of his Third District as follows:

> *"I have made a canvass of my district, and I find the term of years that the keepers and surfmen average in that district is a trifle over five years for all of them. I find that seven men, including the district superintendent – that is myself – have served a period of twenty years and over, and but seven; and I have written a hurried sketch of each of these surfmen and of myself, which I would like to present to the committee as evidence of their faithfulness in the service and of the character of the work that they have done. I have a list of over 600 wrecks here in my pocket, which I have compiled from memory and records of the Service to show what we have done in the third life-saving district – that is, what was then a branch of the third lifesaving district. That is, the Long Island district and the Rhode Island district were one at one time, but I have confined myself to these records of wrecks that have occurred within the scope of my present district, including a part of Fishers Island – that is, the eastern extremity of it, Block Island, Point Judith, Beaver Tail, and Newport – and these seven men who have served twenty years or more are directly or indirectly connected with nearly all of these wrecks that I have in this list. I have three stations on Block Island, which is a summer resort and a fishing camp, and the men there in the fall and winter make anywhere from $10 to 860*

a week cod fishing in smacks. In the spring those that want to, and do not like to go fishing, have all the work they can do in getting the hotels ready; and during the summer months they have teams and pleasure boats that earn them a great deal more money than they can get in the Life-Saving Service. At Newport there is one station where the conditions are equally bad. It is only about twenty minutes drive to the city, and the best of the men get positions running launches and running pleasure boats and at other work, and that is the way that we have lost the best of our men in the district, who have taken those positions. At Fishers Island, I have had the pay roll from that station, which is the only official document since the 25th of last month. That is an island by itself, and they depend upon their own efforts. The crew go over from the mainland, and the first part of last month there was not a regular man on duty: they were all substitutes. Watch Hill is a summer resort and fishing resort. There is no better place in the country for both for those men to make a livelihood.

Narragansett Pier is another place where we have a station, and Point Judith is the last, and of all places it is termed as a fog hole on our coast charts, and a man never goes there that he does not see the bones of some good vessel. It might be considered the worst station we have. We have had more than 200 wrecks on Block Island since the Life-Saving Service was established, as you can count up from this list. One of those seven men whom I have mentioned, including myself, is surfman No. 1 on the Block Island Station. He was too old and infirm for appointment as a keeper when the change was made. I found it necessary, in making the change for the betterment of the Service, to put in a No. 2

man who was a much younger person and better qualified to help out in the work. That No. 1 man has done valuable service. I have a little sketch of his life right here. The keeper at the New Shoreham Station is a man 65 years of age. He has been in the Service about the same length of time that I have, perhaps thirty-one or thirty-two years, and he has done much valuable work during that time, and of course he can not stay in much longer. A man 65 years of age cannot expect to remain in much longer. I have mentioned two out of those seven men.

The keeper of the Brenton Point Station has been in the Service thirty years. He sat at the table with me at Point Judith for eleven years, and I do not think any man of his age, unless it is myself, has been to more wrecks than he has, and we have been to a great many together. This man, Capt. C.C. Kenyon, the keeper of the Brenton Point Station, saved the Government about $20,000 in one fire at his station, and he was unmercifully burned, but he saved the building; and the report which I made in 1904 is here, together with a little sketch of his life and two photographs showing the station and barn that he saved, and showing the condition that he was in from his burns. The night I was there and nursed him he was unable to see out of any eye, and I never saw a fireman burned so badly as that man that was not a corpse, and nobody else ever did, I think."

An Oddity

One oddity gleaned from reports that is worthy of mention is the endorsement of a remedy called "Pain-Killer" as reported in the Woonsocket Reporter December 22, 1894.

"What it means to be a Surfman; Hardship and Injury is his Chief Reward.

One midwinter night in a blinding snowstorm, Captain Arthur L. Nickerson in command of the gallant schooner Allen Green ran out from Vineyard Sound before a northeast gale and made for open sea. The storm was at its height when the winds shifted so suddenly that the skipper realized that he was caught in the sound of breakers booming on Point Judith's treacherous shores.

Fifteen minutes after the schooner struck, Captain Herbert Knowles and crew of hardy life savers began the work of rescue. Captain Nickerson when brought ashore was in pitiable condition. As he later stated in his official report of the disaster made to the superintendent of the Life-Saving Service. "I suffered much from cramps and pain caused by the bruises I received before I went ashore, having been at the wheel fifteen hours continuously."

The life savers wrapped the brave sailor in warm blankets and gave him "Pain-Killer" freely. The famous old remedy accomplished immediate relief and Captain Nickerson slept as peacefully as a child that night and awoke next morning in a condition to face another tempest, if necessary.

He feels that prompt use of "Pain-Killer" after his fearful experience rescued him from unutterable suffering and even saved his life. Brave Captain Knowles is now the assistant superintendent of the district. He says the life savers all use "Pain-Killer" and consider it the best and most reliable "all around" remedy they can have by them.

Captain Asa Church of Point Judith Station; Albert Church of Narragansett Pier, Davis at Watch Hill, Saunders at Quonochontaug and their gallant crews, endorse Captain Knowles and his unstinted praise of Pain-Killer as an invaluable remedy for emergencies encountered in daily life."

3 The Rhode Island Stations

Chapter 4
The Block Island Stations

By far, more shipwrecks and marine disasters took place around the waters of Block Island than any other location in Rhode Island. A complete listing of shipwrecks could never be compiled, but attempts have been made to identify those that have been reported. *B.W. Luther*, a diver and marine historian, has charted the locations of over 200 shipwrecks around Block Island. Due to the high number of shipwrecks occurring around the island, the U.S. Life-Saving Service recognized the importance of this area. The severity of losses was so disastrous that three life-saving stations were eventually established around the island, and the position of Assistant Superintendent of the Third District was established. *Nicholas Ball* was assigned to the island and stationed in New Shoreham. The salary of the Assistant Superintendent paid by the Service in 1887 was set at $500 per year.

The northern end of pork chop-shaped Block Island is called Sandy Point and it sits only 8.8 miles from Point Judith. The island is 5.1 miles long and 3.1 miles wide. It is dominated by high cliffs on the southeast corner, while its northern sandy point dips low and disappears into the sea forming a shoal reef that captures the unwary navigator. Centered somewhat midway between Montauk Point at the eastern end of Long Island, New York and the entrance of Narragansett Bay, Block Island and its rocks and shoals are both navigation landmarks and hazards to coastal shipping.

The island sits in the middle of a navigational traffic zone and divides the waters into Block Island Sound on the northwestern side and Rhode Island Sound on the north eastern side. The two most dangerous areas are Sandy Point's underwater bar and Southwest Ledge's breaking seas off the island's southwest shore.

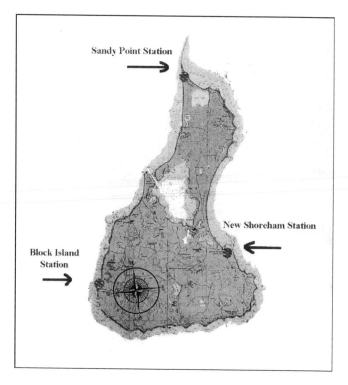

Locations of the three original life-saving stations on Block Island

As for the Island itself, in 1876 *Rev. Samuel Livermore* of Block Island wrote:

> *"No person ever saw the surface of the ocean more uneven than the land of Block Island, excepting those who witnessed the flood in the day of Noah. Imagine then several tidal waves traveling in the same direction from*

west to east each rising 150 feet above the level of the sea and their bases nearly touching each other and on the tops sides and intervals "chop waves" in every conceivable shape and position covering completely the tidal waves; and when the reader has done this, he has an outline of the view from the observer's eye who stands in good light."

The Island was a navigational landmark for vessels transiting west heading into Long Island Sound, or outside to New York City during the era of coastal schooners and early steamships. Vessels sailing east were charting coastwise for destinations in Buzzard's Bay or around Cape Cod and Nantucket Shoals to Boston and posts along the northern Atlantic coast. Some considered Block Island itself a navigational hazard sitting in the middle of a heavily traveled commercial coastal shipping lane. The 17-mile Cape Cod Canal was not completed until 1916 and even then, Block Island was a landmark to set a course to steer for or to clear the islands of Martha's Vineyard and Nantucket. East/west coastal schooner ships arriving from Europe and from other offshore locations steered for Block Island's Southeast light as a confirmation of their first landmark approaching the continent.

Shipping disasters were almost a way of life on the island. They were recorded as early 1690 and some developed into colorful legends. One of the most popular was the demise of the vessel *Palatine Light* on December 27, 1738. The ship had crossed the Atlantic from a Baltic port and Block Island residents knew she would be passing nearby. The *Palatine* was carrying religious refugees from Germany. The islanders had experienced a bad winter and were starving,

4 Block Island

so they plotted to misguide the vessel, ground her and then loot whatever was available from her holds. False signal lights were burned and the *Palantine* came ashore near Sandy Point. Firebrands were launched, setting the vessel aflame and passengers jumped to their deaths into the rough surf.

As the *Palantine* broke apart, the islanders found nothing but rotten food and most alarming, dead passengers who were relatives of Block Islanders. One of the survivors, a self-proclaimed witch, placed a curse on the islanders telling them that they would forever see a burning ship off the point with the crying sounds of those who perished. The eerie tale of a fiery ship that has supposedly appeared off the coast of Block Island on and off for centuries is now considered one of the ten best Rhode Island ghost stories.

Versions of the story apparently were generated by an actual disaster of the vessel *Princess Augusta* carrying 300 or so passengers from Amsterdam, The Netherlands to New York. Over half of the passengers including her captain died during the crossing. Ninety or so survivors came ashore when she wrecked on Block Island.

Other stories about the *Palantine Light* exist; all with a different twist and different dates, yet reports of a ship on fire on the horizon coupled with ghosts still excite the island population.

It was reported that on two different occasions, once in the 1850s and the other in the 1840s, six vessels came ashore on a single day. The annual Life-Saving Service reports, beginning in 1872, show numerous losses and strandings.

These disasters were so frequent that *Samuel Truesdale Livermore* wrote in his history of Block Island:

> *"A visitor here can hardly turn his eyes without having in sight pieces of wrecked vessels, used for posts in fences, gates, and for hitching horses, and in buildings. Nearly all the harrows of the Island have teeth made of ship-bolts. The posts of a long piece of fence near Sandy Point are from the timbers of vessels. A catalogue of all (who) grounded here during the past century, would doubtless approach, or perhaps, exceed a thousand in number."*

Indicative of the frequency of shipwrecks was the establishment of two wrecking company businesses on the island. The Old Protection Wrecking Company of Block Island, and the New Wrecking Company. Their sole business was to salvage the remains of vessels, their cargos, rigging, and machinery to sell for profit on the mainland. Equipped with pumps, pulleys, heavy hawsers, windlasses, empty casks (used for floatation), wrecking tools and tugboats, they often succeeded in re-floating a wreck and towing it to Newport, Rhode Island or New London, Connecticut. It was risky business where there was always the possibility of losing their own property, their lives, and failing to get the wreck into port. Payment was only made if they succeeded in any particular venture.

Not all went well with the wreckers, as often bargaining was required with the stranded ship captain. However, once the vessel was abandoned, Admiralty Laws of high and low order determined how wreckers claimed rights to the vessel and its cargo. In most cases there was much risk involved. Few of these wrecking companies were possessed with the skill or courage necessary in the dangerous work. The duty of the Life-Saving Station crews on the other hand, as their name implied, was to save lives. Other than their small boat handling experience, they never were equipped to handle movement of large vessels and rigging, nor save cargo. As a result, a shipwreck salvage company became a lucrative, if not somewhat a shady, business.

As ship wrecks increased, Block Island gained further notoriety as a Rhode Island ship graveyard. There were rumors that the wreckers from time to time set up false and erroneous lights to guide ships off course and onto the shoals. Once aboard, anything that was moveable was stolen. The wreckers claimed they were honest Christians, baptized in the island's church and never the ones who participated in these devilish deeds. Their notoriety grew with more incidents supposedly caused by islanders. A false ship with masts, rigging and sails was constructed near Sandy Point to disorient navigators and lure ships toward the shoal. This may not be completely true, but wrecking companies were ready to strip bare any vessel that was stranded and abandoned.

Two lighthouses had been built at each end of Block Island to warn navigators of this large mass of *terra firma* bisecting the seaway, North Light (1829) and Southeast Light (1875). The famous Southeast Light's base sits 150 ft above sea level on a cliff of Mohegan Bluffs. It is equipped with a first order Fresnel lens, the brightest and largest lens available with a range of 24 miles (30 miles on a clear night). No other light in Rhode Island has a lens as powerful or as bright. It presently shines an emerald green flash every 5 seconds. North Light was built on the low strip of Sandy Point's beach to warn of the dangerous underwater finger shoal that harbored the graveyard for those who erred. The white flashing light sits 58 ft above sea level with a range of 13 miles. North Light was built and rebuilt four different times. Two additional lights were later added at the breakwater entrances of Old Harbor and New Harbor (Great Salt Pond).

Three life-saving stations were established on Block Island: Block Island Station (1872) on the west side near Dickens Point, New Shoreham Station (Old Harbor, 1874) and Sandy Point Station (1898). Sandy Point Station was only 500 ft north of North Light Lighthouse. Six surfmen were assigned to each station from August 1 to May 31. One additional man was added from December 1 through April 30. Lookouts were stationed each day at the station location, and at night surfmen walked the beach looking for vessels in danger or ones that were stranded. During the summer months of July and August all three stations were shut down and the crews were placed on leave with the exception of the keeper.

Life-saving operations were shifted to the new Block Island Station located just inside the entrance to Great Salt Pond on the western side of the island when the Dickens Point, New Shoreham and Sandy Point Life-Saving Stations were permanently closed. That station today operates primarily in the summer as a Search and Rescue base. It opens on Memorial Day weekend and operates until the end of the first week of September. The Coast Guard has stated that: "During the winter months there is less traffic at sea, so the Block Island Station duties are transferred to Station Point

Judith 12 miles to the north." They remind all mariners in Block Island Sound to report marine emergencies to the Command Center at Coast Guard Sector Southeastern New England using VHF marine radio channel 16.

The following sections within this chapter provide more descriptive information on each Block Island station and include details of selective shipwrecks and related marine disasters along with the actions taken by the station crews.

Block Island Station LSS #5
Coast Guard Station #62

Station Block Island was the first station established on Block Island. It was provided for by Congress in March 1871 and constructed in 1872. It was followed by the New Shoreham Station (1874) and by the Sandy Point Station (1898). Block Island Station was built on Block Island's west side near Dickens Point and originally named Block Island Southwest Point Station. Coast Guard records state it was located on the west side of the island near Dickens Point, but its actual location was at 41° 09'40"N, 71° 36'40"W, a quarter mile north of Southwest Point near the end of Cooneymus Road.

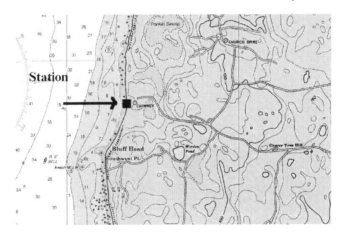

Twelve miles of water lie between the southwest side of Block Island and Montauk Point, New York. While there is ample water depth between the two, numerous shoals, ledges and bottom features cause tremendous breaking seas in bad weather, particularly over "southwest ledge", which lays three miles from Block Island. Block Island Channel is the seaward entrance to Block Island Sound and Long Island Sound, and at time rages with white water. The winter gales with strong northeast or northwesterly winds were the causes of most of the disasters that Station Block Island addressed. Large sailing vessels caught in this passage during gale force winds from the northwest were often restricted in maneuvering, and often forced to run before the winds, meeting their fate on the west shore of the island.

The station was reconstructed in 1886, and later enlarged using a Bibb design #2. Fifty years later, in 1936, its operations were moved into new expanded facilities at the inside entrance of Great Salt Pond. At that time the station had consolidated all of the Coast Guard's operational responsibilities of the island, including those of the two other life-saving stations at Sandy Point and New Shoreham.

After Block Island Station near Dickens Point was decommissioned, the building and property were eventually purchased by a private owner who refurbished the building for use as a private home.

Left: Block Island Station crew with Assistant Third District Commissioner Nichols Ball in background   *Photo USCG Historian's Office*

Right: Later image of Block Island Station Bibb #2 type design, now a private residence   *Photo website Southport Marketing Inc.*

Remarks:

Noted Rhode Island Life-Saving Service historian *Tim Dring* wrote:

> *"Station Block Island, as originally established by the USLSS, was located a little above the southwest corner of Block Island (41°09'40"N/71° 36'40"W) but, with the introduction of motorized rescue craft was re-located to the current site inside the entrance to Great Salt Pond (41° 11'40"N/71° 35'20"W). The station at the Great Salt Pond location was commissioned in January of 1936, and by December of 1941 had the following rescue craft assigned: 36 ft. 8 in. Type TR motor lifeboat No. 4756/CG36400, Type S pulling surfboat No. 3854/CG25370, and 38 ft. cabin picket boat No. 4303/CG38317. The new Station Block Island consolidated the Coast Guard's operational responsibilities and resources for the entire island, which had previously been split between the three original USLSS stations locations: the original Block Island station, New Shoreham, and LSS Sandy Point. Station Block Island was discontinued as a year-round, fully active unit in 1986. Currently, Station Point Judith, RI provides either a 27 ft. rigid hull/foam collar SAFE type medium utility boat, or a 25 ft. Response Boat-Small during the summer boating season as SAR detachment. This detachment no longer operates out of the "Roosevelt type" station building (which was turned over to the Block Island municipal government by 1990) but, rather, operates out of a smaller building located just a short distance away, with its dock also located in Great Salt Pond."*

In 1988 the Coast Guard ended its year-round operations at the Station and limited them to the summer months only. In 1996 the Station's buildings were given to the Town of New Shoreham with the stipulation that they keep quarters for the Coast Guardsmen on duty during the summer.

Keepers (*information from the USCG Historian's Office*)

The first keeper of Block Island Station was *Samuel Allen*. He was appointed at the age of 46 (with 30 years surfman experience) on December 12, 1872 and served until January 16, 1878. He was followed by *Edward C. Allen*, who was appointed at the age of 52 effective January 16, 1878. The date of the end of his service is unrecorded. Next came *Samuel Allen, Jr.* who was appointed October 25, 1879 and served until he was discharged on November 25, 1886.

Nathaniel D. Ball succeeded *Allen*. He was appointed December 6, 1886 and resigned for physical reasons on January 31, 1905. *William Teal* followed him on January 21, 1905. He became incapacitated and retired on December 2, 1922. Then came *Arthur L. Lanphere* who was reassigned from the Maddeket Station (Martha's Vineyard, MA) on August 26, 1928 and reassigned to the Gay Head Station (Martha's Vineyard, MA) on November 2, 1931. Chief Boatswains Mate *H.E. Johnson* relieved him. *Eli Sprague, Jr.*, took command on April 15, 1933. He had come from the Green Hill Station and served until his retirement on December 1, 1935. Then came Chief Boatswains Mate *H.B. Peterson*, followed by *Harry E. Johnson*, who was reassigned from the New Shoreham Station on July 15, 1937.

Surfman *Charles H. Mitchell* was singled out during congressional hearings in 1908 as an example of one of the crewmembers at Station Block Island.

"Surfman Charles H. Mitchell, surfman No. 1 of the Block Island life-saving crew, was born on the island March 2, 1855.

HE entered the Service at the Block Island Station (west side of the island) September 1, 1887, since which time he has taken an active part in more than one hundred wrecks of nearly every description that are forced ashore on that part of the island, imperiling the lives of several hundred.

In his early life he was a shore fisherman, and the type of surfmen that made up the crews at the stations in the early eighties.

His Qualifications as a surfman in connection with his willingness to faithfully perform all duties assigned to him, together with services of the past should be recognized by Congress. A person at his age (52) afflicted with rheumatism, with a family to support, bearing the record he does, is worthy of special recognition by all fair-minded persons."

Selected Events Recorded in Annual LSS Reports (Modified for Clarity by the Author)

1878 The Event of the Schooner *Rebecca A. Huddle*

During the night beach patrol on September 1, 1878 the schooner *Rebecca A. Huddle* of Philadelphia, with a crew of seven, was found stranded on the western shore of Block Island. While the west side of the island is rocky, there are spaces of beach and she fortunately stranded off one of them. It was dense fog at 10:30 PM when the vessel struck. Wind was light and there was no surf or surge. She lay there until the following day when she apparently got off with no damage.

1879 The Event of the Schooner *Eliza A. Hooper*

This event was somewhat unusual as the vessel involved was one employed in salvaging shipwrecks.

The winter of 1878-1879 was not something the crew of the schooner *Eliza A. Hooper* would soon forget. Out of Camden, New Jersey, she had earlier in December stranded near Jones Inlet, Long Island and had got off only after a wrecking company was hired to drag her off the beach. During a northwest gale and freezing temperatures less than one month later on January 3, on her way to New York in charge of eight wreckers, she came ashore two miles north of the Block Island Station. Arriving on location, the surfmen found three members of the crew had used the schooner's boat and landed on the beach. The life-saving crew brought ashore the other five who were left aboard. The vessel eventually was saved.

1880 The Event of Schooner (*Name Unknown*)

One important role of the night beach patrol was warning ships of impending danger. April 3, 1880 is a prime example. Although the name of the vessel was not recorded, prevention of grounding, saving the ship, cargo and possibly lives, took place. At 4:30 AM the surfman from this station sighted a schooner running free with the wind and headed to run ashore. He burned his Coston light and signaled them by waving his lantern. Almost immediately the vessel's crew were made aware of their danger and they hauled off to windward evading the potential disaster. This type of action was repeated year after year throughout the life of this station and all of the others.

1884 The Event of Schooner *Bradford C. French*

Each event and each action by Keeper *Samuel Adam Jr.*, who was in charge of Block Island Station for seven years from 1879 to 1886, had some uniqueness associated with it.

In May of 1884 the schooner *Bradford C. French* was stranded off the west coast of the island during foggy and rough sea conditions. Keeper *Adam* and crew boarded the schooner, asking the crew if they wanted to abandon ship. The crew was unwilling to do so and remained aboard until the following morning when winds and seas increased to the point that the ship and crew were in danger. The life-saving crew returned to the schooner, saved the nine-man crew and boarded them at the station for two days. There is no mention of the method used to remove the crew off the vessel. Keeper *Adam* then found free transportation for the crew to Newport. Two weeks later the schooner was floated by a wrecking crew and towed to Fall River. Two years after this rescue (1886), *Adam,* for reasons unknown, was discharged from his duties.

1887 The Event of Rower *Wolf*

On the cold winter day of February 1, 1887 a man named *Wolf* was found by the station's beach patrol. He had been rowing a small boat that came ashore on Block Island 1½ miles north of the Block Island Station. The man was in route from Fall River, Massachusetts to Norwich, Connecticut and being without a compass, found himself lost. (There is no explanation as to why he was rowing some 80 miles down Narragansett Bay across Block Island Sound to go up the Thames River and found himself so far from the coast line on the west side of Block Island.) His hands were badly frostbitten and he suffered from exposure to the cold. He was taken to the station and cared for with food and shelter. Nearly a week later he left for home, very grateful for the attention and kindness shown to him.

1893 The Event of the Coal Barge *Reliance*

As an introductory note regarding schooner barges; they were commonly large old sailing vessels "metamorphosed" into transports carrying coal after they were no longer useful as sailing vessels. The strains of tall masts and sails were reduced to two short masts and just enough sail area to give them headway, and then they were towed by steamers with inexpensive crews on board which made economic sense to their owners. In the late 1800s this class of vessel was in high demand and their use increased. Unfortunately most were rotted out, not fully seaworthy and near the end of life.

In the early afternoon of February 20, 1893 during gale force winds, the large coal barge *Reliance* was cut adrift between Montauk Point and Block Island by the steamer having her in tow. She drifted onto the west side of Block Island and went to pieces within the hour. Five persons were on board, three men, a boy and a woman. Four of them appeared to have been washed overboard and drowned. The fifth was torn away from the rigging about ten minutes after hitting the bar. The *Reliance* was loaded with 1,450 tons of anthracite coal bound from Philadelphia to Boston. She was rigged with two shortened masts and reduced sail. She was not designed to be a seagoing vessel wholly dependent on her sails, but rather accustomed to be towed by a steamer; in this case the *Panther*. The master of the steamer had rounded Montauk Point in a gale from the west and both vessels encountered tremendous waves. The steamer's decks were smashed and she was taking on water. When the steamer slowed down, the *Reliance* forged ahead, at which time the master gave the order to cut the towing hawser. *Reliance* fell into the trough of the sea and drifted helplessly toward the shore of Block Island. The south surfman patrol at Block Island Station sighted her three-fourths of a mile off shore, but she was obscured by both snow and huge "waves of solid water" which rolled over her. The station beach apparatus was run out to the point where they expected the schooner to strike. The station crew from the New Shoreham Station was also summoned. *Reliance* struck four hundred yards from the beach and the inconceivable fury of the storm began to tear her into pieces. They tried to save the one man sighted on board who was in range of the Lyle gun. Keeper *Ball* trained the Lyle gun and fired, but it fell short. Several more shots were made in the succeeding minutes, but none of them reached the wreck. The man on board made an effort to reach the rigging just as the barge split into two parts and all was lost. Winds were clocked at 65 mph and the temperature ranged from 10-15° F. The surf was so rough that all agreed, including twenty witnesses, that the surfboat could not have been launched.

1894 The Event of the Schooner *Bradford C. French*

During foggy and rough sea conditions on May 6, 1894 the Life-Saving crew of Block Island Station found the schooner *Bradford C. French* stranded off the beach nearby the station. The crew of nine men, including the master, refused to abandon the vessel with hope that seas would calm and she could be towed off into deeper water. The following morning the seas increased and endangered those on board. The life-saving crew succeeded in landing them safely. There is no record of how they were removed from the vessel. After two days of being housed at the Station the crew was provided free transportation to Newport. Seven days later the schooner was released by the wreckers and towed to Fall River for repairs

1910 The Event of the Fishing Dory (no *name*)

Swamped dories were not uncommon incidents in Rhode Island waters. While designed to ride in high seas, and in most cases handled by experienced seamen, high-sided New England dories do indeed swamp when heavy seas broach over their gunwales. While this report does not explain if the dory belonged to a mother ship or was launched by local fishermen from shore, it does highlight the dangers of rough seas and the risks fishermen were exposed to.

This boat contained four fishermen who were swamped one-third of a mile southwest of the Block Island Station. The life-saving crew went to their assistance in the motorized surfboat. One fisherman had swum ashore, but when the surfboat arrived on the scene another man was struggling in the water and two men were clinging to the overturn dory.

The surfboat was backed into the surf and the man in the water was picked up. While this rescue was being performed, one of the men clinging to the dory was washed off the boat. He was sinking when a surfman thrust a boat hook within his grasp and he was hauled aboard. With the third man also in the surfboat they returned to the station where restorative treatment was given to the rescued.

1911 The Event of the Schooner *Mary Adelaide*

One of the most frustrating rescues experienced at the Block Island Station took place on December 28, 1911. A four-masted schooner, *Mary Adelaide Randall*, registered in Port Jefferson, New York, with a cargo of coal bound from Norfolk, Virginia to New London, Connecticut, caught herself in a strong northwesterly gale. Driven further east and unable to come about, she grounded onto the rocky ledges on the west side of Block Island below Grace Point. Keeper *William Teal's* beach patrol discovered the *Randall* in poor visibility. She was headed toward the shore and the patrol surfman lit off his Coston signal light and called the crew of the station. The vessel had already hit the rock ledges a quarter of a mile off shore and was beginning to break up when they arrived. She filled quickly and sunk. Keeper *Teal* was unable to reach the vessel and deferred further actions until daylight. Both the stations at Sandy Point and New Shoreham were contacted for assistance, and by the time they arrived many townspeople had gathered to watch the attempted rescue.

Time after time the surfboat crews tried to launch boats, but were either turned back by the high surf, or capsized and thrown along the beaches. The crews were wet and cold and exhausted. The Lyle breeches buoy gun was loaded with the largest charge they had, but it failed when fired against the strong wind, and fell less than half way to the *Randall*. The lifeboat crews again tried to reach the vessel and finally succeeded to get along side. The crew, one man at a time, dropped into the boat and all ten were successfully landed on the beach. The *Randall* was a total loss. Keeper *Teal* served seventeen years at Station Block Island until he was classified "incapacitated" and retired in 1922.

New Shoreham Station USLSS #4
Coast Guard Station #61

The New Shoreham Station was established in 1874 on the east side of Block Island, near the breakwater near the landing at 41° 10'30"N, 71° 33'07"W. A new site was acquired and the station was rebuilt in 1887-1888. It was later moved to 41° 10'20" N, 71° 33'30"W in 1915.

The site was decommissioned on July 15, 1937 and hence abandoned. In 1947 its historical significance was recognized and in 1968 Mystic Seaport acquired the building.

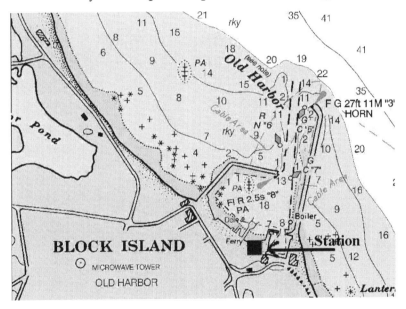

Remarks:

This station was built on Block Island's east side, near the breakwater in 1874. The breakwater was started in 1870 and was built to provide a safe harbor for the ferryboats frequenting New Shoreham, and as a secure refuge for vessels. At that time, it was one of the most extensive engineering works undertaken in New England, reaching 1,250 ft on one leg and containing 85,000 tons of rip-rap. The basin created by the breakwater provided safe anchorage for vessels. The basin was completed in 1879 and was the main harbor for the island. It is still used today as the primary destination for ferryboats.

The station was originally called the Block Island (Northeast Side) Station. The original site became inadequate due to changing conditions and a new site was acquired in 1884. The station buildings were moved in 1885 and the station was rebuilt in 1887-1888. A contract was awarded in 1921 for repairs and remodeling of the station building. The station was decommissioned on July 15, 1937. The original building was sold at auction, used as a stable and later a blacksmith shop; and then again moved to the west side of the island to be used as a club house. In 1968 the Mystic Seaport acquired the building and transferred it in its entirety to their museum site as an historical artifact.

New Shoreham Station building currently on display at Mystic Seaport, Mystic, CT.　　　　Photo courtesy of Richard Sullivan

After the decommissioning of the New Shoreham station, its "duties and responsibilities were taken over by the new Roosevelt type station built inside the entrance to Great Salt Pond on west side of the island". (Information courtesy of *Tim Dring* and the July 16, 2005 online edition of the Block Island Times.) *Dring* notes that the station was the last original Life-Saving Station to be in operation on Block Island.

Keepers (*information from the USCG Historian's Office*)

The first keeper of the New Shoreham Station was *Nicholas Ball*. He was appointed on September 2, 1871 and served until appointed as Assistant Third District Superintendent on August 4, 1875. He was also a U.S. congressman and instrumental in having the New Shoreham building built. Then came *William P. Card*, who was appointed on September 2, 1875 and resigned August 20, 1881. He was followed by *Ralph E. Dodge* (appointed September 2, 1881 until his dismissal December 21, 1885); *Darius B. Dodge* (December 21, 1885 until his resignation February 2, 1889); *Amazon N. Littlefield* (July 27, 1889 until he "died from disease contracted in line of duty" on March 18, 1914); *Eli Sprague, Jr.* (May 6, 1914 until reassigned to the Green Hill Station on February 21, 1928); and *George W. Streeter* (from the Brenton Point Station on February 21, 1928 and reassigned to the Watch Hill Station on April 17, 1929). Next came *Chief Petty Officer S.E. Littlefield* in 1929 (reassigned from the Brenton Point Station), who was commissioned on December 29, 1931 and reassigned to the Third District Office on April 15, 1933. Chief Petty Officer *H.E. Johnson* was commissioned on May 10, 1935 and next took command of the Station; he subsequently was reassigned to command the Block Island Station on July 15, 1935.

During congressional hearings in 1908, Keeper *Capt. Amazon N. Littlefield* was singled out as an exemplary crewmember at New Shoreham Station.

> *"Keeper Capt. Amazon N. Littlefield was born on Block Island February 28, 1843. He entered the Life-Saving Service November 15, 1876 as surfman No. 6 at the New Shoreham Station, and later was promoted to the position of No. 1. He was also promoted to the keepership of the same station August 3, 1889. (During which time he has taken part in more than a hundred different disasters, and while in command was successful in many timely rescues, such as the saving of the crews of the O.R.M. Mowry, Vamoose, U.S. naval tug Leyden, and many others, as shown by records of the Service. He is in his sixty-fifth year of age. Though agile for a person of his age, his past services have earned him a retirement seat with a worthy and a liberal pension."*

Selected Events Recorded in Annual LSS Reports (Modified for Clarity by the Author)

1878 The Event of the Bark *Hesse Darmstadt*

On November 8, 1878 *William Card*, keeper at New Shoreham Station, observed a three-masted bark burning torch lights on deck about one mile from his station. He assumed the vessel was in need of assistance and responded by sending up a red rocket followed by a Coston signaling immediate help was available. The station crew launched their surfboat, and within a half hour they were able to board the vessel. It turned out to be the British bark *Hesse Darmstadt* out of London, England on route to Providence with a cargo of scrap iron. The *Hesse Darmstadt* was signaling for a pilot and was not in distress. Keeper *Card* loaned the captain a chart of Narragansett Bay along with some sailing instructions and that was all that was needed.

1885 The Event of the *Anna B. Jacobs*

This event highlights the difficulties of both the circumstances that challenged the life-saving crews, and also how extreme weather conditions cause hardships. It begs understanding of why and how these underpaid hearty men were so committed to their tasks.

On March 20, 1885 at 5:00 PM, during a furious northwesterly gale, the schooner *Anna B. Jacobs* of New York dragged afoul of the breakwater while lying in New Shoreham Harbor. She had recently arrived with a load of stone for the improvement of the breakwater. The place where she struck was 500 yards from the life-saving station. Keeper *Dodge* and crew saw what happened and put off in the surfboat to her assistance. The winds were so strong that their first attempt failed. It was so intensely cold, that in a short time the men's fingers were frostbitten and the boat was covered with ice. They returned to the beach, loaded the boat on the beach carriage and hauled it over the beach well windward of where the *Jacobs* lay. They made a second attempt and successfully anchored the surfboat by veering a cable close enough to the schooner to take her crew of five safely in the surfboat. All survived, although everyone was drenched with ice cold water and frost. A nearby schooner, the *R.H. Daly*, took the crew aboard for the night. The following morning the gale had subsided enough for the life-saving crew to ascertain the schooner's condition and they found her stranded with the stern damaged. The captain of the schooner was advised to get a wrecking company, but could not agree on terms. The captain of the *Daly* offered help. The life-saving crew from the Block Island Station had arrived by that time and also offered assistance, but to no avail. The schooner filled with water and sank. The following day with all hands manning manual pumps, they tried unsuccessfully to float her, but the only course left was to call for steam pumps from the Newport Wrecking Company. They arrived, pumped her out and towed her to Newport for repairs.

1885 The Events of the *Lizzie D. Barker*, *Lelia Linwood* and the *William A. Oaks*.

During a northeasterly gale on June 5, 1885, three vessels parted their cables and were driven ashore into New Shoreham Harbor. The first was the vessel *Lizzie D. Barker*. Both the New Shoreham and Block Island Stations were closed for the summer, but Keeper *Dodge* gathered a crew, manned the surfboat and, in three trips, brought 15 men with their baggage safely ashore. They were sheltered at the Station for two days until the vessel got off.

Lelia Linwood came ashore close to the station and struck a ledge. A sail was hoisted and she was carried over the reef to an area with a smooth and sandy bottom. Twelve of her crew landed in her own boats and were provided shelter at the New Shoreham Station overnight.

Next was the schooner *William A. Oaks* of Gloucester, also with a crew of 15 men. They too landed in their own boats, but the captain refused to leave his vessel. Ten of the crew were accommodated at the station, joining the others. The off duty Block Island life-saving crew who volunteered to help their brethren at New Shoreham also stayed the night. The storm abated the following day and local wreckers with special devices got the three schooners afloat. The *Barker* was heavily damaged and taken to Newport for repairs.

1886 The Event of the Dead Body of *Miss May Hatch*

Not all of the events of the life-saving station were associated with strandings or sinkings. Herewith is the brief story of a body found at sea.

On June 18, 1886 the dead body of *Miss May Hatch* was found twelve miles south of Block Island by the fishing schooner *Laura Louise*. The body was brought to the New Shoreham Station. She was a young lady drowned at sea from the steamer *Chatham* on June 16. The remains were kept at the station until June 20 and were then sent to relatives in Baltimore, Maryland.

The following letter was received at the office of the Superintendent.

> *"June 21, 1886: Dear Sir, Please accept thanks of the family for the prompt service given our letter of request concerning the recovery of the body of Miss May Hatch. We cannot forbear to express our gratitude and appreciation of the readiness which the Service placed at our command.*
>
> *Very Respectfully, Wm. M. Hatch"*

1893 The Event of the Schooner *William G.R. Mowry*

The brief written report (without details) of the disaster of the *William G.R. Mowry* exemplifies the over simplification of a written record of an event which took place at the New Shoreham Station:

> "Dec 5, 1893. Stranded during a snowstorm 4 miles from the station. With the beach apparatus landed the crew of six men in safety; cared for them at the station."

There is no record of the name or disposition of the schooner. What we do know is the surfmen had to make a four-mile trek during a snowstorm (Sandy Point Life-Saving Station had not yet been established), hauling the beach cart along in beach sand, and probably also the surfboat. In any event, it was an arduous task getting there and to launch a line, rig the hawser and breeches buoy, and then land and rescue six men. The crew was also cared for at the station for several days. This written report, among other reports, is representative of significant understatements of the actual events and actions taken.

1894 The Event of the Brig *Nellie Pickup*

Another incident in March 1894 demonstrates the service provided by the New Shoreham Station. The brig *Nellie Pickup* was anchored dangerously close to shore. She had mistaken shore lights and was burning signals for assistance. Keeper *Ralph E. Dodge* launched the surfboat, boarded the brig and stood by in case the wind blowing on shore should freshen and cause further concern. A tug was called and when she arrived the station crew assisted heaving up the brig's anchors to get it underway.

1894 The Events of the Gale of October 10

On October 10, 1894 the Life-Saving crew at New Shoreham Station were almost overwhelmed with the catastrophes brought about by a gale that raced across the island, and by the physical feats they performed that day.

At 3:20 AM the schooner *L.O. Foster* mistook the light at the outside of the breakwater because of heavy seas and poor visibility. She stranded in the shallow water and launched distress signals. The patrol alerted the station crew and a boat was launched immediately. On the way out they met the four crewmen and transported them to the station for refuge. Some cargo was recovered along the beach, but the *Foster* was a total loss.

While picking up what they could from the *Foster's* cargo, the crew witnessed that the catboat *Bessie Fisk* had parted from her moorings in the harbor, come up hard on the beach and was being pounded by the surf. The crew rigged tackle and hauled her further up on the beach where she lay safely and secure from possible destruction.

Later the sloop *Lizzie* parted her cables in the outer harbor and was stranded while a heavy sea was running. The seamen rowed out to assist the crew, secure her sails and then made a hawser taut to her masthead to prevent the rolling sea from breaking her mast. The crew of three was taken off and provided both food and shelter at the station.

The last rescue of the day was the schooner *Maria* who was first lying on the weather side of the breakwater during the storm and only 20 ft from the rocks. Her cables had parted earlier and only a single chain held her in place. The station crew boarded her to carry another line, but found nothing long enough for the purpose. A strong hawser from the station was then carried aboard and the *Maria* was wrapped around the breakwater and hauled into the basin where she was secured.

1898 The Event of the Schooner *William Rice*

During the morning of May 24, 1998 the schooner *William Rice* was stranded on Sandy Point (the Sandy Point Life-Saving Station was not yet in operation). Word was passed down to the keeper at the New Shoreham Station by the North Light keeper. Keeper *Amazon N. Littlefield* of the New Shoreham Station hired a team of horses and conveyed the surfmen to area. A surfboat was stationed there near the lighthouse for just this purpose. Upon launching the boat and boarding the schooner they found the master and crew lightening the vessel by throwing over her cargo of lime in hope that the vessel would float off at the next high tide. The surfmen joined the act and despite unloading tons of lime, the *William Rice* still was bound to the bottom. The master then called for two tugs to get her off, but due to threatening weather no help arrived. The crew of the vessel, along with the surfmen, continued throwing 800 barrels of lime overboard and by the next high tide the now badly leaking schooner floated free. The master requested the surfmen stay with him to land his men if need be. The surfmen remained onboard until the schooner had reached Race Rock Light the following morning, a distance of about 18 miles away, where the master thought he would be able to carry on without them. The surfmen ended up sailing to New London,

Connecticut and back to the New Shoreham Station via Newport.

1889 The Event of the Schooner *Josie Reeves*

The captain of the schooner *Josie Reeves* that was in danger of dragging anchors wrote to the Chief of Life-Saving Service the following:

> *"Sir Allow me to extend my thanks to you as Chief of the Life-Saving Service of this country, especially in behalf of captain D.B. Dodge and his crew of the New Shoreham Station, who have rendered the very valuable service on two occasions. Once on February 25, 1880 when we were ashore near the breakwater at Block Island we probably would have lost the vessel had it not been for the prompt action of the captain and his crew. And the other on January 9, 1889 when captain Dodge and his men boarded our vessel, which we had brought to anchor a short time before the breakwater. We were dragging off and would probably have gone to sea not been for their prompt aid and assistance in helping us safely into the harbor. I feel its my duty to extend my sincere thanks to you in appointing a man like captain Dodge to the position he now holds, as I consider him very competent and capable in every respect, and I trust that when help is wanted you will find him ever ready to help, aid, and assist all who should call upon him, or in any way need his services.*
>
> *I remain your obedient servant,*
>   *Vincent C. Smith, master schooner Josie Reeves"*

1898 The Event of the British Schooner *Vamoose*

One of the larger vessels to come ashore on Block Island was the three-masted schooner *Vamoose*. The stranding took place on December 5, 1898 during a strong northeast gale three miles north of the station. The captain, *Byron Knowlton*, and mate, *H. Brooks*, were washed overboard and drowned.

The *Vamoose* was on route from Cape Brenton Island to Saint John, New Brunswick. She encountered a series of vicious storms, including a cyclonic tempest that drove her far off course by hundreds of miles to the south. She was seeking refuge in the vicinity of Long Island Sound. For over 15 days she had been at the mercy of heavy seas and a succession of gales. In poor visibility, driving westward under double-reefed sails and flying jibs, she struck hard along the beach above Clay Head with seas sweeping over her. The captain saved himself on the top gallant forecastle, and the rest of the crew leapt into the mizzen mast's rigging. Winds by this time were clocked at 60 mph at Block Island. Within ten minutes, captain *Knowlton* was washed overboard and never seen again. Shortly thereafter the mizzen topmast was carried away and the mate *Brooks* fell and disappeared into the raging surf.

As the vessel began to break up, the remaining crew attempted to make a raft and two crewmembers *(Webb* and *Christiansen)* luckily made it ashore, but were thought to have drowned by the crewmen still aboard the vessel. Being half frozen to death, the two crewmen managed to climb 90-100 feet to the top of Clay Head and reached the house of Mr. *Samuel L. Harper*. *Harper* dispatched his son to the New Shoreham Life Station with the news. The wreck, however, had already been discovered by the north patrol. Keeper *Amazon Littlefield* of the station secured a team of horses to pull both the beach cart and the surfboat four miles to the *Vamoose* which was lying 120 yards offshore with the four men still aboard clinging to the mizzen rigging. Lowering the surfboat down the steep face of the bluff was accomplished, but it soon was apparent the boat could not safely be launched among the rocks and heavy surf. The breeches buoy was then deployed and the first shot fell through fractured the deck. The second shot was successful and with great resistance due to the current, surfmen waded waist deep into the breakers to clear the fouled line from the rocks.

The four remaining crew aboard the *Vamoose* were rescued without delay. Twenty minutes after the last man was saved, the mizzenmast fell and the stern of the vessel broke away. It was noted that the disaster took place outside the limits of New Shoreham's night patrol where a new life-saving station (Sandy Point) was under construction.

The final testimony of the event was the appreciation letter to Superintendent *Sumner Kimball* dated December 6, 1898:

> *"Sir: the undersigned, survivors of the British schooner Vamoose wrecked under Clay Head Bluffs at Block Island last Sunday night, desire to testify their heartfelt gratitude to the crew of the New Shoreham Life-Saving Station, who by their brave, plucky work saved us from sure death. Our thankfulness for their work and our appreciation of their kind of treatment at the station later on, will never be forgotten.*
>
> *Charles N. Adams, Second Mate*

> Charles Mitchell, Steward
> Samuel L Webb, Seaman
> Hands Christiansen, Seaman
> Samuel Taylor, Seaman
> Carl Baggidge, Seaman
> Of the wrecked British schooner Vamoose"

1899 The Event of the Sloop *Sunny Side*

While not as dramatic as the disaster of the British schooner *Vamoose*, the November 21, 1899 letter from the master of the sloop *Sunny Side* indicates the supporting assistance the Station provided to vessels in distress.

> "Dear sir; I should like to praise the services rendered to me by Captain A.N. Littlefield and crew of the New Shoreham Station, Block Island, on the night of September 11, 1899 when I went ashore in the south east gale of wind. I had hardly had struck the beach when the patrol was at hand and helped me and the crew worked hard and faithfully for three days succeeded in getting the sloop-smack Sunny Side afloat, saving her and her cargo of fish. I can further state that you have a good crew and a gentleman for captain of the lifesavers. They made me quite at home in their house and also helped me make repairs so that I could get to New London. I wish you would compliment them for the work they did for me.
>
> Very respectfully,
> Charles Kessler, Master of sloop Sunny Side"

1903 The Event of the U.S. Navy Steamer USS *Leyden*

On January 21, 1903 in thick fog, the 35-ton USS *Leyden* was stranded 200 yards from shore and one mile west of the Southeast light, Block Island. The ship was sighted at 12:40 PM by the light keeper who then notified the New Shoreham Station keeper of the grounding by telephone.

The New Shoreham Station called on the crew of Block Island Station to go to the scene and pulled their own surfboat and beach apparatus to the shore abreast the wreck, where the two crews united. Upon arrival they found seven of the steamer's crew attempting to land in the vessel's lifeboat that was dashed to pieces on the rocks by heavy seas. The men, however, safely reached the shore with a line from the vessel and assistance from on-lookers. The surfmen sent the breeches buoy whip out by the steamer's line, rigged the breeches buoy and landed the 29 men still remaining on board without mishap. Each man was taken to the light keeper's house for shelter. Afterwards, the rescued men were taken to the life-saving stations where needed dry clothing was supplied from the stores donated by the Woman's National Relief Association. The following day, the men from the USS *Leyden* were transported to Newport. The vessel, which had served in combat during the Spanish American war, was a total loss.

The acting Secretary of the Navy *Charles H. Darling* wrote to the Secretary of the Treasury:

> "*I cannot speak too highly of the promptness and efficiency of Captain Littlefield and a crew of the New Shoreham Life-Saving Station, who in 45 minutes after they heard of the*

grounding got their gear over 3 miles of very bad roads and in an hour from the time they got the alarm and landed the first man; nor of Captain Ball and the life-saving crew of the Block Island Station who came to assist. The men of the Leyden landed cold and wet with only the clothes they had on. They were at once sent to the South East Light when they were most kindly received and looked out for by keeper Dodge and Mrs. Dodge and assisted by assistant keepers Clark and Westcott and Mrs. Clark and Mrs. Westcott. Half of the men that night were housed by keeper Dodge and the other half sent to the New Shoreham Life-Saving Station.

The Navy Department desires to thank the Treasury Department and the services rendered by its above mentioned employees and desires to express its appreciation of the efficient manner in which their duties were performed.

Very respectfully Charles H. Darling Acting Secretary."

1904 The Event of the Sloop *Theresa*

Events of this type were common where no loss of life or cargo resulted.

BLOCK ISLAND, RHODE ISLAND, *September 15, 1904.*

DEAR SIR: I wish to thank the keeper and crew of the New Shoreham Life-Saving Station many times for the service rendered me on September 15, 1904. At about 5 a. m. the wind blew a gale of 84½ miles an hour, by signal-service register, and my vessel, the sloop *Theresa*, of New London, dragged both anchors to the breakwater, and would have been a total wreck had it not been for the strict watch kept by Captain Littlefield and his men. The watch saw the vessel and reported to Captain Littlefield almost as soon as she struck, and they came like firemen to a fire. The captain and part of his crew boarded my vessel, putting out our anchor as they came aboard, and in less than ten minutes from the time they boarded the vessel she was afloat, and hung safely by the Government hawser. There was a sloop passing us in the gale (American sloop *Bessie*), which was saved by the surfmen, and her owner also wishes me to thank you for the service rendered by your gallant officer and men. The part of the crew not with the keeper were doing great work where men of the best experience were needed at that moment. They saved thousands of dollars worth of property from loss, and you could hear the praises on all sides of the work the life-savers had done.

I will say good-bye, sir, with many thanks from many a captain, as well as myself and crew.

I remain, your servant,
R. A. SANCHEZ,
Master Sloop Theresa.

Hon. S. I. KIMBALL,
General Superintendent Life-Saving Service.

1905 The Event of the Steamer *Spartan*

At 4:15 AM on March 19, 1905 the 222-ft long steamer *Spartan* was en-route from Providence to Philadelphia and became stranded in dense fog on the reef almost under Southeast Point's Lighthouse located one and three-quarter miles from the Life-Saving Station. She was built at Wilmington, Delaware in 1883 and displaced 1,596 tons. Even though the light and fog signal at the lighthouse were working, the steamer went on the rocks on a rising tide. The Station's life-savers launched the surfboat and went to her assistance. At the time, the sea was smooth and as such, their assistance was declined because the master felt confident he could work the vessel afloat at high water.

At nightfall a heavy swell developed with signs of threatening weather and the sea began to pound her sides and break on board, sweeping her decks fore and aft. The crew became apprehensive of her breaking up and going to pieces during the night. Signals of distress were hoisted and the Station crew responded by taking 11 of the ship's crew ashore in the surfboat and sheltering them at the station, while the rest of the crew stayed aboard. Near midnight winds increased to 25 mph and heavy seas built up, crushed her bulkheads and the hull filled with water.

Steamer Spartan aground on rocks below the Southeast Lighthouse before she broke up.   Post card LaBelle

All hope of saving the vessel was abandoned, and at daybreak the station crew saved six more of the crew by surfboat. By afternoon the only hope to save the four remaining crewmembers was by the breeches buoy. A line was shot from the Lyle gun, the breeches buoy apparatus rigged and the remaining crew rescued. The *Spartan* continued to break up and proved to be a total loss.

1905 The Event of the Tug *Bluejay*

On the early morning of December 16, 1905 the tug *Bluejay* encountered a northeast gale. The vessel had damaged machinery and was cast upon the east side of Block Island at about 2:30 AM. She was shortly discovered by a beach patrolman who hastily retraced his steps and alerted Keeper *Amazon N. Littlefield*. The station crew boarded her and brought the master safely to shore. The engineer had managed to reach land before the arrival of the station crew. The *Bluejay* was eventually floated free and taken to port for repairs.

The master of the tug responded to the service provided with the letter below:

> *"I wish to extend my thanks to the captain and crew of the New Shoreham Life-Saving Station at Block Island for their heroic work in rescuing us from the tug this morning when we might have perished, not only for the rescue but for the treatment shown us at the Life Station. It was different from the action of coastwise steamers who passed us from time to time, seeing our signals of distress, but ignoring them and simply leaving us to perish. Vessels came up and spoke to us and then went on their way. But we were saved.*
>
> *John P. Brown Master, Tug Bluejay"*

Sandy Point Station USLSS #60

The Sandy Point Life-Saving Station was established in 1898 on the north side of Block Island, near the lighthouse. Coordinates are 41° 13'40"N, 71° 34'40"W. The original position was listed as "on Block Island, north end, near light". The station was decommissioned in 1922.

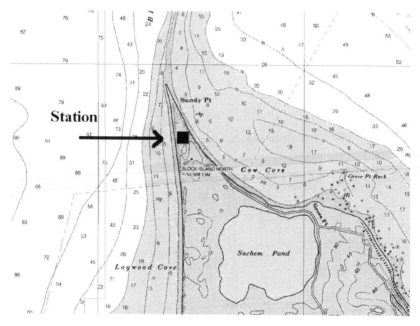

Remarks:

The Sandy Point Life-Saving Station occupied land slightly north of the Block Island North Lighthouse by permission from the Lighthouse Service. The Life-Saving Station was built in 1898 and placed in operation in 1899.

Sixty-nine years earlier, in 1829, the federal government built Block Island's first lighthouse on Sandy Point. Four lighthouses have since been built at this location. The present lighthouse, the North Light, was built in 1867 and is open to the public for tours.

The extreme north end of Block Island is a slim finger of sand called Sandy Point. As the end of the land tapers into the sea, an underwater shallow sandbar of about four feet depth continues out over a half mile. It is named North Reef and its shallow depth has been the cause of hundreds of strandings in rough weather. Any vessel finding itself aground in this area gets pounded by relentless breaking seas. A quarter-mile north another shallows with depths less than 16 ft adds to the danger. In addition to the shallow reef is the constant crosscurrent of up to 3 knots as each tide change rushes east or west. The lighthouse was established in December 1829 and did help avert some disasters, but the wrecks and strandings continued. The lighthouse was built and rebuilt three additional times enduring countless storms while ships still misjudged the location of the shoal. Wrecks occurred quite frequently and finally in 1898 a life-saving station was established 500 ft north of the lighthouse. Certainly the occupants of the lighthouse, who for years lived alone and remote from other humans on Block Island, welcomed the surfmen of the Life-Saving Service as new neighbors.

Keepers (*information from the USCG Historian's Office*)

The station's first keeper was *Edward P. Sisson* who was appointed on November 29, 1898 and served until October 10, 1904 when he was reassigned to the Fishers Island Station. After *Sisson*, the keepers were *Simon R. Sands* (appointed October 6, 1904 and served until appointed as Assistant to the District Superintendent in Portsmouth, New

Hampshire on July 22, 1915), *John E. Tourgee* (acting until appointed January 20, 1916 and reassigned to the Bay Shore Station on February 9, 1919), *Oswald A Littlefield* (acting until his appointment and then immediately reassigned to the Watch Hill Station on July 12, 1919), and *Clarence E. Peckham* (acting until his appointment on May 18, 1920 and then reassigned to the Fishers Island Station).

For reasons not explained, the station keeper position was vacant after that period and the station was discontinued in 1922. Nevertheless, *Amos P. Tefft* was reassigned from Point Judith on June 24, 1922 and served until he retired on December 27, 1927. The station was again listed as discontinued and disappeared from the listings in 1928.

Sandy Point Station 1907 with crew

Building design identical to the 1891 Quonochontaug Station

With the station in operation only 29 years, Sandy Point Station dealt with a considerable number of wrecks compared with other Rhode Island stations. The Larchmont disaster on 1907 (see Chapter 1) and its notification by a young man survivor who came ashore half frozen to death to alarm the world of vessels sinking gave the station its notoriety.

A statement by District Superintendent *Knowles* in 1908 when asked about the personnel turnover at the station replied: *"At Sandy Point Station, on Block Island, which was manned in the winter of 1898 or 1899, perhaps January, 1899, or somewhere thereabouts, there is only one man now of that original crew. They were a model crew of young men. Every man who went on there had bright prospects of becoming a No. 1 surfman. We have lost them all but one."*

Selected Events Recorded in Annual LSS Reports (Modified for Clarity by the Author)

1899 The Event of the Brig Barge *Plover*

While all the details are not recorded, the large vessel *Plover* stranded near the Sandy Point station at 9:15 PM on November 4, 1899. The situation was serious enough that the station's beach apparatus was deployed and located abreast of the *Plover*. The gear was set up and a line fired successfully across her. The first man of the six-man crew came ashore 1½ hours later via the breeches buoy. The master and mate remained aboard, not desiring to abandon the vessel to wreckers. The following morning the master was landed by the breeches buoy and made contact with local parties to float the brig. Seven days later she was successfully floated.

1910 The Event of the Schooner *W. Talbot Dodge*

A furious gale from the northeast coupled with a blinding snowstorm stranded the auxiliary schooner *W. Talbot Dodge* off Sandy Point. She was found by the surfman on patrol a half mile southeast of the station on December 6, 1910 at 9:00 PM. He summoned the life-saving crew and they arrived at the site opposite the vessel and successfully fired two shots from the Lyle gun across her. Apparently the crew of the vessel made no effort to retrieve the shot lines, perhaps because breaking seas now covered her entire deck. The life-saving crew shouted instructions above the winds and noise to the onboard crew to fasten a line to their dory and drop it into the sea. The dory came ashore and the life-saving crew attached a line to it and shoved the dory back into the sea. The dory was hauled back and forth by means of two lines between the ship and shore until all hands were safe ashore. The schooner was a total loss.

Chapter 5
Watch Hill Station USLSS #3
Coast Guard Station #58

At the very southwest end of the state of Rhode Island, a stubby promontory of beach called Watch Hill Point juts into Block Island Sound. The Point, along with a 1½ mile curved finger of sand identified as Napatree Beach, breeches a body of water called Little Narragansett Bay. These features join together the three states of Rhode Island, Connecticut and New York (Fishers Island). The rocks, shoals and tidal currents off these locations were magnets to ship disasters as commercial shipping used the passages as highways for delivering passengers and cargos to and from bustling 19th century New England towns and cities.

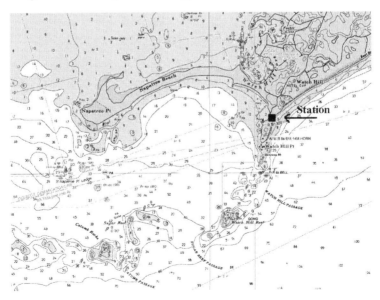

5 Watch Hill

Watch Hill Point with its rocks, reefs and shoals has always been notorious for shipwrecks. It was the prime reason to establish a lighthouse there in 1808. The light was Rhode Island's second lighthouse, built after the Beavertail Lighthouse that is located at the entrance of Narragansett Bay. Beavertail is America's third oldest lighthouse, constructed in 1749. Watch Hill light was one of America's first lights that "eclipsed", using a rotating clock mechanism. Its first lighthouse keeper, *Jonathan Nash* of Westerly, remained there for 27 years. During that period of time he recorded 45 shipwrecks.

An early volunteer-staffed life-saving station of unknown origin was established at Watch Hill Point in 1850. However, it was not until one of Rhode Island's deadliest marine disasters on August 30, 1872 that the U.S. Life-Saving Service decided to establish a new station.

The nighttime disaster in dense fog was a collision between the passenger liner *Metis* (Neptune Lines), destined to Providence from New York City and the schooner *Nettie Cushing*. The collision took place less than a mile from Watch Hill Point at 3:40 AM. The bow of the *Nettie Cushing* cut deep into the *Metis*, inflicting a fatal wound. The *Metis* was holed and almost immediately began sinking with 149 people on board. Survivors, some swimming and others clinging to debris rafts and a lifeboat off her deck made it to shore. Local residents hand-in-hand made a human chain and pulled passengers from the surf onto shore. The station's volunteers, including the Watch Hill Lighthouse keeper, launched their 21-ft lifeboat and rescued those still alive in the water. Some reports state 85 people were rescued from the sinking vessel by boats that rushed to the scene, but 67 souls perished in the storm-tossed sea. Her remains now lay in 135 ft of water.

The 1878 Annual Life-Saving Service Report mentions that three new life-saving stations were authorized by the Act of June 18, 1878; one of the three was Watch Hill. This station replaced the early 1850 volunteer station. Watch Hill Station, designated Station #3 by the Life-Saving Service was located three sixteenths of a mile north of the lighthouse, midway along the beach strip to the village at 41° 18'20"N, 71° 51'30"W. The building was completed in 1879. Twenty-eight years later, in 1907-1908, the station was rebuilt in a configuration of newer design identified as a Port Huron house. This design included a very large three-story octagonal lookout tower protruding directly up from the center of the building structure. The boathouse was a detached building adjacent to the house. Watch Hill disappeared from the list of stations in April 1947. According to USCG records the station was decommissioned in 1947.

5 Watch Hill

Watch Hill station with 1876 type station house designed by J. Lake Parkinson with an open lookout tower   USCG

Watch Hill Station crew hitched to beach cart   Photo courtesy Knowles file

5 Watch Hill

Watch Hill crew 1904   *Photo courtesy of USCG Historian Office*

Watch Hill rebuilt in Port Huron style; post 1900
Photo courtesy of Longo

5 Watch Hill

Keepers (*information from the USCG Historian's Office*)

The first keeper of the Watch Hill Station was *Joshua P. Clark*, who was appointed on November 9, 1878 and served until his resignation on August 18, 1881. He was followed in turn by *James A. Barber* (August 11, 1881 until he was dismissed June 15, 1883), *John F. Mash* (July 2, 1883 until he resigned August 15, 1891), *Walter H. Davis* (November 23, 1891 until his retirement on October 31, 1916), *Howard Wilcox* (reassigned on November 13, 1916 from the Quonochontaug Station and reassigned to the Office of the Third District Supervisor in Wakefield, Rhode Island on July 5, 1919), *Oswald A. Littlefield* (reassigned from the Sandy Point Station on July 12, 1919 and reassigned as Assistant to the District Supervisor in Portsmouth New Hampshire on April 3, 1920), *Amos Broadmeadow* (reassigned from the Fishers Island Station, New York on May 18, 1920 and was transferred to the position as Assistant to the Third District Supervisor on April 17, 1929), and *George W. Streeter* (reassigned from the New Shoreham Station, he retired on April 1, 1932). Next came Chief Boatswains Mate *A.E. Newcomb* in 1932. He was relieved by *Arthur E. Larkin*, newly reassigned from the Quonochontaug Station on April 15, 1933, who subsequently went to the Old Harbor Station on April 6, 1934. The station was next commanded by two chief boatswains mates, *E.F. Sanborn* in 1934 and *S.K. Gamache* in 1935.

During congressional hearings in 1908 Keeper *Walter D. Davis* was mentioned as an example of one of the crewmembers at Watch Hill Station:

> "*Capt. Walter H. Davis, keeper of the Watch Hill Life-Saving Station, was born in the town of Stonington, New*

London County, Conn., August 15, 1865 and was a fisherman by occupation.

He entered the Service at the Watch Hill Station as surfman No. 1 of the crew on October 20, 1886 and during the summer months (inactive season) was captain of a fishing vessel. He was promoted to the keepership of the station November 25, 1891 (succeeding Capt. John F. Nash, resigned), a position he now holds. He has figured in perhaps nearly a hundred rescues, both in the vicinity of the station and those having occurred on the reefs about the eastern extremity of Fishers Island, in which many lives imperiled were saved.

He is energetic, and his twenty-one years of heroic work in the Service has brought him many favorable comments which are recognized by the public and officers of the Service. His character, courage, and qualifications are exceptional. Though but 42 years of age he has seen much of the Service, is a model keeper, and but few are his peer or can show a better record."

Selected Events Recorded in Annual LSS Reports (Modified for Clarity by the Author)

Watch Hill Station over the years witnessed many shipwrecks and her life-saving crews diligently responded whatever the event and under all possible weather conditions imaginable. The chronological events below represent a sample of incidents experienced at that station.

1879 The Event of the Schooner *John Mayo*

To move in and out of Long Island Sound ships have to navigate through shallow reefs that extend southwest of Watch Hill Point to Fishers Island. These reefs are not only treacherous because they rise only a few feet below the surface of the water, but also because the flood and ebb of the tide though the eastern end of Long Island Sound creates rip currents that exceed 5 knots. The buoy system must be adhered to exactly if entering or leaving Stonington, Mystic or New London, Connecticut. There is no room for error. An example of what can go wrong is the incident of October 26, 1879 when the early morning station patrol at 5:45 AM discovered the schooner *John Mayo* of Lincolnville, Maine bound for Mystic, Connecticut hard on Watch Hill Reef. The reef is located only a half mile off Watch Hill Point and the lighthouse. The passage through the reefs southeast of the point requires local knowledge and is known as a dangerous area. The life-saving crew immediately launched the surfboat and boarded the *John Mayo*. Her cargo consisted of lime and she had a crew of three men. Finding no towing hawser aboard, they returned to the station, procured a towing hawser and rowed back to throw overboard 250 barrels of lime to lighten ship. At the next high tide she floated off.

1882 The Event of the Schooner *Momento*

A similar incident took place on November 18, 1882, this time in falling snow. Another schooner, *Momento*, bound from Perth Amboy to New Bedford sought refuge in Stonington, Connecticut during a storm. The crew of four was displaying distress signals. It was 8:00 PM and the signal was acknowledged by the life-saving watch who burned a Coston signal in reply. When they reached her by the surfboat, *Momento* was leaking badly alongside the reef, her sails were blown away and her small boat stove in and useless. The life-saving surfmen took the crew ashore, lodging them for the night. The next day they boarded the vessel, found water above the floor boards and assisted pumping her out until a tug arrived and towed her away.

1882 The Event of the Schooner *Open Sea*

Napatree Point and its low 1½-mile barrier beach lie at the south side of Little Narragansett Bay and were part of the night watch patrol area. At 3:30 AM on December 16, 1882 a surfman discovered a vessel lying off the Point, but could not distinguish if it was at anchor or on the reef. He burned his Coston light, but received no answering signal. Keeper *James A. Barber* was summoned and although there was a strong west wind and heavy seas, he ordered the surfboat launched to confirm that the vessel was on the reef. She was the schooner *Open Sea* of Belfast, Maine on route to Providence with a cargo of coal and five crewmen on board. The crew and their baggage were taken aboard the surfboat and to the station where they were housed for a day and a half. *Open Sea* pounded herself on the reef and was a total loss along with her cargo.

1885 The Event of the Schooner *Wave*

Watch Hill Station, as all the other life-saving stations in Rhode Island, was closed down during the summer months. This did not deter responding to the need for help if a surfman was nearby. As happened in August 1885, a small government schooner, the *Wave,* bound from Newport to New London misjudged the buoy off the narrow channel of Watch Hill and struck the rocky reefs about a third of a mile from the closed station. Keeper *John F. Mash* was out fishing that day and went to provide assistance. The crew of the vessel had lowered their sail and attempts to heave her off were not successful. Keeper *Mash* told them to raise sail that helped heel the boat over and she handsomely came off. *Mash* then piloted the vessel into the channel and saw her safely on course up Fishers Island Sound.

1885 The Event of the Schooner *Vraie* and Schooner *Hope Hayes*

On January 11, 1885, the schooner *Vraie* of Dighton, Massachusetts with a crew of six aboard and loaded with coal from Baltimore, was trying to enter the harbor at Stonington, Connecticut. Running with only headsails, the ship ran aground on Penguin Shoal. The shoal is located near Wamphassuc Point (the western side of the Stonington Harbor). The Watch Hill life-saving crew hastened to assist her, helped raise all her sails, wing-on-wing, and with the rising tide forced the vessel over the shoal and piloted her into the harbor. The incident was caused because the navigation buoy marking the shoal was not been in the proper place.

Eleven days later, the schooner *Hope Hayes* of Bath, Maine with seven men on board was sailing from New York to Boston loaded with a cargo of "fustic". (Fustic is a bright yellow dye that is very colorfast when used with a mordant.) It is frequently combined with other dyestuffs and various mordants to produce a range of yellow and greenish colors.)

In somewhat thick weather, *Hope Hayes* struck on Catumb Reef. The reef, now called Catumb Rocks, is a mile southwest of the Watch Hill Station and lies in the middle of a confusing chain of rocks and shoals stretching across the entrance of Fishers Island Sound. Today, the passage to and from the sound is well buoyed, but tides and current require attentive navigation and a sailing vessel sailing in poor weather is easily waylaid onto disaster.

The station crew at Watch Hill observed the *Hope Hays* almost as soon as she had struck launched a boat and found the crew at work throwing cargo overboard to lighten her. An anchor kedge was run off her stern and the hawser hauled taut to prevent the vessel crabbing further onto the reef. The sails were then guyed flat aback and all hands set to on the cargo until forty tons had been jettisoned. By that time the tide had turned and the schooner was backed off the reef, but she was leaking so badly that two pumps had to be manned. Keeper *John Mash* took charge, tripped the anchor and piloted the vessel into Stonington Harbor with two feet of water in her hold. To save the *Hope Hays* from sinking in deep water, she was purposely moored next to a wharf where she could lay aground, until all her cargo was discharged in preparation of hauling her out on a railway for repairs.

1885 The Event of the Sloop *Hadley*

The sloop *Hadley* sailed out of New London on October 5, 1885 with a crew of two men. Beating down Little Narragansett Bay the vessel mis-stayed while attempting to come about, and before steerage was recovered had drifted onto Seal Rock, northwest of the station about a mile and a

5 Watch Hill

quarter. The keeper saw her, and with four of his crew they rowed out in the surfboat to help her. The sloop had put out an anchor, and with help of the life-saving crew she was hauled afloat without damage, hoisted sail and piloted safely out of danger.

1886 The Event of the Schooner *Olio Ochilcott*

Life-saving attempts on wrecks were not always successful, as in the instance of the schooner *Olio Ochilcott* hailing from Ellsworth, Maine on the morning of January 9, 1886. The Swedish mate was tossed into the sea after she had grounded. The account below is recounted from the 1886 *Life-Saving Service Annual Report*:

> "The mate, a native of Sweden, named K.J.B. Hagland, was drowned as soon as she struck. From the accounts received the man's death was clearly not chargeable to remissness on the part of the Service. The schooner was on her way from Clarke's Island, Maine, to New York with a cargo of granite, when overtaken by the terribly disastrous easterly gale and snowstorm of January 8 and 9. She was making for Watch Hill Channel in an endeavor to reach the shelter of Stonington Harbor, in Fisher's Island Sound, or the safer haven of New Loudon, a few miles beyond, when the ominous roar of the surf burst upon the ears of the startled crew. It was then about 6 o'clock, but the morning was so intensely dark and the snow so thick and blinding that it was impossible to distinguish objects twenty yards away. The helm was instantly put hard down in an effort to luff to the wind and claw off, but it was too late, and before the vessel could respond she was in the breakers. The captain, seeing that she must strike, and that it would be impossible to remain on deck, called to his subordinates to take

to the rigging. This warning was not a moment too soon, for they had scarcely reached the main rigging when the schooner thumped on the bottom, and she was immediately boarded by the seas, which completely buried her in a smother of foam, the spray from which flew half-mast high. In fact the men, when but twenty or thirty feet from the deck, narrowly escaped being washed away. The mate, who was uppermost, suggested that they move up into the cross-trees, and the poor fellow was about doing this when the schooner took a sudden plunge shoreward and struck a second time with such force that the shock literally flung him from the rigging into the angry waters beneath, and he was swept out of sight. He disappeared in a moment. It is a wonder they were not all thrown off. The two others succeeded, however, in gaining the crosstrees, and as the vessel became steady, as she filled with water, they were comparatively safe. The schooner had stranded about a mile and three-quarters east of the Watch Hill Station, (Third District.) and was discovered an hour later by the east patrol (Surfman Clark) as he returned over his beat to the station. Clark immediately hurried forward with the alarm, and in half an hour the crew were on the way with the beach-apparatus. It was a toilsome drag through the deep snow drills, but with the aid of a team, which the keeper sent for upon setting out and which joined them when half way, the place was reached at 1 o'clock. The schooner lay head on, about two hundred feet from the shore, with the surf breaking all over her. The first shot carried the line forward of the foremast and over the jib-stay, where it could not be reached. At the second fire the line passed between the fore-topmast and the backstays, and lodged on the spring-stay. The sailors got hold of it and hauled the whip out as far as the fore cross-trees, where the block caught, and they could not dislodge it. The lines were therefore hauled back by the station crew and a third shot fired. This time the line passed between the masts and fell on the captain's arm, as lie reached out to catch it. The distance being short the whip and the hawser were soon rigged, and in half an hour from the time of the station crew's arrival the two survivors were drawn safely ashore in the breeches-buoy. They remained at the station for several days, until the cargo was recovered and the wreck stripped of rigging and sails."

1886 The Event of the Schooner *John Crockford*

On August 9, 1886 at 3:00 AM, the schooner *John Crockford* stranded near Napatree Point, a mile or so westward of the Watch Hill Station. She had a crew of four and was bound from Providence to Stonington, Connecticut laden with kerosene. She had run too close to the Point in the darkness. When the anchor was dropped to check her, the stock of the anchor broke and the ship was at once forced ashore by the heavy seas. As the station was closed for the summer and the crew all off duty, the vessel was not discovered until daylight. Keeper *John F. Mash* mustered a volunteer crew as quickly as possible and went to her relief. She was lying on the beach with an ugly sea breaking under her stern, which made the situation serious. *Mash* set to work without delay and carried out a stern anchor with the surfboat. After about 2½ hours of hard heaving at the windlass, the relief party succeeded in getting the schooner afloat in a leaky condition. She was at once piloted out into deep water on her way to Stonington a few miles distant.

1886 The Event of Fire on Shore

The Watch Hill crew on many occasions assisted with emergencies in town. In this case, on September 15, 1886, it was a fire that had broken out in the town at 3:30 AM. The beach patrol sighted the flames and called in the alarm. The promptness of the crew no doubt prevented a serious conflagration. The scene of the fire was a drugstore and a photography gallery. The crew arrived in only a few minutes, running from the station with all of the fire buckets available. Although they were unable to save the building, they succeeded in quenching the flames that had just broken out in the adjoining structure, thus preventing the fire from spreading any further.

1886 The Event of the Schooner *Fred F. Carl*

The incident of the schooner *Fred F. Carl* on December 8, 1886 conveys the catastrophic situation that can arise from a combination of gale force winter winds, ice and a foolish attempt by members of the ship's crew who returned from shore back on board their stranded vessel.

Summoned by telephone in the Watch Hill Station, the crew manned their surfboat and responded to the call for help by rowing eight miles eastward to assist the lighthouse tender *Cactus* in an attempt to float the schooner *Fred F. Carl* of Belfast, Maine. She had stranded the previous night on Quonochontaug Beach located halfway between Watch Hill and Point Judith. The schooner was from the island of the Buen Ayre off the coast of Venezuela, and carried a cargo of salt and redwood for New York. She had been blown off course by strong westerly gales, and the weather was so cold that she was covered with ice, and in that condition unmanageable. She had on board a crew of eight men. When found, she could not be gotten off and operations were suspended for the day. The captain took passage to New London on a wrecking tug while the rest of the crew landed on the beach and found shelter in a farmhouse. The following day the station crew was again called to the wreck to rescue the mate and two seamen who, heedless of the danger of such an undertaking, had returned to their vessel and spent the night on board. With the weather again in stormy state, they found themselves in great peril. Before the life-saving crew had reached the scene, they had obtained the assistance of horses and proceeded as expeditiously as possible. The three crewmen attempted to land in their own boat, but the boat capsized and two of them, the mate and one of the seamen drowned. The accident was caused by the mate who unwisely cut the line that connected the boat to the shore. Immediately upon doing so, the boat swung broadside to the sea throwing them into the surf where only one of them reached the beach. Had they taken to the rigging until the lifesavers arrived 1½ hours later, they would all have been saved. The schooner *Fred F. Carl* was a total loss, as was most of her cargo.

1886 The Event of the Schooner *C.W. Locke*

> *"Shortly after 7 o'clock on April 15 in the evening during thick fog, the beach patrol of Watch Hill Station discovered a schooner ashore at Napatree Point a mile and a half westward of the station. As soon as the patrol surfman could return to the station the crew turned out in their surfboat to her assistance. She was the C.W. Locke of*

Harwich, Massachusetts with a crew of six men with the captain's wife and baby on board bound From New Bedford to New York in ballast. She lay 300 yards from shore and her crew had carried out an anchor in preparation of getting off. The life-saving crew came aboard and helped to heave on the windlass and she eventually pulled off. She was then piloted out into the channel and departed for Fishers Island Sound apparently without damage."

1887 The Event of the Schooner *Vicksburg*

This incident on September 23, 1887 demonstrates the high level of physical endurance of the station crew at Watch Hill. In this case they worked from 7:00 AM until late afternoon of the same day, exhausting themselves from rowing through high seas, manning pumps, helping set sails and then rowing to Stonington, Connecticut, to summon a wrecking salvage vessel for the stranded schooner before returning to their station:

"The lumber-laden schooner Vicksburg of and from Bangor, Maine while on her way to New York through Block Island Sound was struck by a violent southeast squall and being unable to carry sail was put before the wind. The spindle on the east side of Lord's Channel was mistaken for one that marks Watch Hill Reef, and at 7 o'clock in the morning she ran on Meeting House Shoal about 2 miles and a quarter from Watch Hill Station. The weather was thick and rainy with a high sea running. The vessel was discovered by the west beach patrol who hurried to the station with the tidings. As quickly as possible the surfboat was launched and after a hard pull against both wind and tide they found the schooner pounding heavily and

leaking. The surfmen joined the 5 man crew at the pumps and set the schooner's foresail and floated her off the shoal where she was anchored with a broken rudder and five feet of water in her hull. Her disabled condition made it necessary for the lifesaving crew to row to Stonington, Connecticut, a distance of almost 3 miles again in rough seas and high winds to engage a tug. Returning to the vessel, she was found to be completely waterlogged whereas a large wrecking vessel was required to take her inside. The lifesaving crew then returned to their station."

1890 The Event of the Brig *Toronto*

"At forty minutes past 7 o'clock in the evening of November 25 the west patrol of the Watch Hill Station discovered a large vessel close ashore heading directly for the beach. The surfman quickly burned off a Coston Signal and then hastened the alarm to the station life-saving crew. The weather was thick with rain and in the Southeast gale. The vessel Toronto, was a brig from Windsor, Nova Scotia on her way from Sidney, Cape Brenton bound for New York loaded with a cargo of coal. The vessel struck the beach broadside a short distance from the station and lay in a dangerous position close by and northeast of the station. She lay over a hundred yards from shore with heavy surf breaking over her. The station crew hurriedly prepared the beach (breeches buoy) apparatus and got in readiness, but due to the almost impenetrable darkness and breaking surf, the furious onset of waves together with the motion of the vessel made it next to impossible for Toronto's crew to get about the decks and into the rigging. Five times the Lyle gun was shot, the line retrieved and reloaded. On the sixth *attempt the line was finally secured aboard. The gear was then speedily put to work by the station crew and five crewmen were rescued by the breeches buoy. The captain and two mates declined to leave at the time and were landed the following morning while the storm still continued. A quantity of baggage and clothes was also brought off by the apparatus. The Toronto became a total wreck with only her sails and anchor chains being salvaged. The crew was housed at the station for a number of days while the stripping of the vessel was in progress."*

1891 The Event of the Schooner *John Proctor* and the *Alice M. Ridgeway*

Two events within two days of each other (December 9 and 11, 1891) involved two schooners. The *John Proctor* whose master mistook lights and stranded the ship on Wicopest Reef, and the *Alice M. Ridgeway* who sprang a leak. The crew from Watch Hill could not reach the *Proctor* due to heavy weather, and had to wait a day to pick up the master who asked for a tug to tow her to New London. The *Ridgeway* was beached and totally wrecked; with the surfmen saved the crew and some of these men were cared for at the station.

1891 The Event of the Schooner *Maggie Cummings*

On Christmas Day 1891, the schooner *Maggie Cummings* stranded in heavy seas. The station crew launched the surfboat after a severe struggle against wind and sea to save the crew of seven with some personal effects. The rescue occurred moments before the vessel stove and sank. The rescued men were housed and cared for at the station for two days.

1896 The Event of the Schooner *Belle R. Hull*

On February 11, 1896, strained by strong winds and heavy seas, the schooner *Belle R. Hull* was leaking badly. In order to prevent her from sinking, the master ran the vessel toward shore. She was almost waterlogged and heading for the beach when discovered by the beach patrol. The acting keeper at the Watch Hill Station, *Elnathan Burdick*, had the beach apparatus transported to the anticipated point of stranding. Almost at the same time a terrific squall with blinding snow blew away the ship's foresail and jib and she was driven onto the beach a half-mile from the station. The Lyle gun was rigged and fired at once, and communication was established between the ship and the life-saving crew. The master's wife and the five men on board were landed safely by the breeches buoy. Ten minutes after the crew was ashore, the masts of the *Belle R. Hull* went overboard and the vessel was dashed to pieces. The crew was taken to the station and provided with dry clothing and shelter. If not for the prompt response by the lifesavers, it is believed this disaster would undoubtedly have cost the lives of everyone on board.

The testimony by *Bell R. Hull's* master is as follows:

> WATCH HILL, RHODE ISLAND, *February 13, 1896.*
>
> SIR: I wish to give expression to the gratitude I feel to the noble Life-Saving Service, which you, as its chief, have done so much to promote.
>
> At 5 o'clock on the morning of the 11th instant the schooner *Belle R. Hull*, of which I was master, sprung a general leak in a heavy gale and sea, and our only hope was to beach the vessel. She was headed for the shore, where a tremendous sea was running, but soon the jib and foresail were blown away, and death seemed to stare us in the face from all directions; then the mortar cart from the Watch Hill Station was seen, being pulled along the shore at a rapid rate by the crew through the soft sand.
>
> As soon as the vessel struck the beach tremendous waves engulfed her, but the gun was fired from shore and the ropes made fast as instructed. In less than fifteen minutes we were all landed, Mrs. Taylor (my wife) being the first to land in the buoy, and the crew following, one at a time. I was the last to leave, and had barely reached shore when both masts fell and the vessel went to pieces.
>
> I have often read of the heroic feats performed by your noble crews, and I think my wife and crew, as well as myself, owe our lives to the Watch Hill life-saving crew. I can not commend too highly Mr. Elnathan Burdick, No. 1 of the crew, who had charge of the apparatus during the absence of the keeper.
>
> I have written the above with the feeling that if I did not write I would be deficient in gratitude for the services rendered, the promptness of which, no doubt, is due to the efficiency of the chief of the Service.
>
> Most gratefully, yours,   JOHN W. TAYLOR,
> *Master of Schooner Belle R. Hull.*
>
> Hon. S. I. KIMBALL,
>   *General Superintendent United States Life-Saving Service, Washington, D. C.*

1896 The Event of the Brig *Josie*

Stranded two miles west of the Watch Hill Station on September 29, 1896, the brig *Josie* was found full of water and pounding heavily on the rocks in rough seas. A tug had come up on her and had a hawser aboard, but could not release her. As seas increased and were breaking aboard her with great force, the captain and crew of three were taken off in the surfboat with their personal effects and sheltered at the station. The following day wrecking tugs hauled her off and took the vessel to Stonington for repairs, saving part of her cargo.

1897 The Event of the Schooner *Maggie Abbott*

On October 23, 1897 the Schooner *Maggie Abbott* stranded one mile south of the station and was found by the beach

5 Watch Hill

patrol. The surfmen went out to find her leaking badly. The crew tried carrying out anchors to heave her afloat, but were unsuccessful. Both winds and increasing seas threatening her destruction, so the crew and their luggage were taken aboard the surfboat and safely landed on the beach. The master of the *Maggie Abbot* made arrangements with a wrecking company to save all cargo and rigging possible. On November 5 the vessel went to pieces.

1898 The Event of the Schooner *Laurel*

The schooner *Laurel*, with a cargo of stone, stranded on Catumb Rocks on May 25, 1898 at 2:00 AM. The crew burned a signal of distress. The night patrol surfman responded with a Coston light and summoned the station keeper and crew. The crew pulled along side the *Laurel*, helped man pumps and commenced throwing the heavy cargo overboard. As the winds veered southeast, the *Laurel* pounded a hole in her bottom and filled full of water. Seeing the vessel could not be saved, the master asked the life-saving surfmen to help strip the schoonor of sails and rigging. When this was done, the steamer *Amagansett* came along and took the master and his one-man crew to Stonington, Connecticut.

1898 The Event of a Recovered Body

As mentioned previously, not all the incidents associated with the Life-Saving Service were associated with ship wrecks. This is the sad story of a life that was lost with the suspicion of malicious intent.

On August 11, 1898, Keeper *Walter H. Davis* was awakened at 11:30 PM by cries of help from the pier. At the same time the surf patrol also heard the cries, launched a small boat and headed for the pier. They found a woman in the water and pulled her aboard. She was carried to the pier where they used the "Service method" of respiration on her for 1½ hours until a doctor arrived and pronounced her life "extinct". The body had not been long enough in the water to sink. It was thought by many that she had not fallen accidentally. Her male companion had acted suspiciously and was placed under arrest.

1907 The Event of the Schooner *Harry Knowlton* and the Steamer *Larchmont*

As described in Chapter 1, the worst disaster to take place in Rhode Island waters was the collision between the large schooner *Harry Knowlton* and steamer *Larchmont*, unfortunately out of sight of the Watch Hill Station. The circumstances of this tragic loss of life took place on the night of February 11, 1907 when the three-masted schooner *Harry Knowlton* collided with the passenger steamer *Larchmont*. Captain *George McVey* of the *Larchmont* gave the following account of the incident:

> "We left Providence at 7 o'clock. A brisk northwest wind was blowing, and we were off Watch Hill at about 11 o'clock. I had gone below to look over the passengers and freight, leaving a good pilot and quartermaster in the pilot house. I returned to the pilot house, passing through there on my way to my room. Everything was O.K. in the pilot house as I stepped into my room and prepared to retire for the night. Suddenly I heard the pilot blowing danger, and I hurried into the pilot house. There was a schooner on the port and her crew seemed to have lost control of her.

> *Without warning she luffed up and before we had an opportunity to do a thing headed for us. The quartermaster and pilot put the wheel hard aport, but the schooner was sailing along under a heavy breeze, and in a moment she had crashed into our port side, directly opposite the smokestack."*

The turbulent waters soon separated the two vessels, which both began taking on water. The schooner, with its crew manning her pumps, was able to stay afloat until it reached a point a few miles west of Watch Hill, where the crew abandoned ship and rowed ashore in a lifeboat. Those aboard the steamer were not as fortunate. Most passengers had retired for the evening, and so those who were able to reach the lifeboats were not properly clothed to face the freezing temperatures. Of the estimated 157 passengers and crew on the steamship, only nineteen survived, and many of these were severely frostbitten and had to have fingers, hands and even limbs amputated.

1918 The Events of the Freighter *Onondaga* and Fishing Steamer *George Hudson*

On June 28, 1918, the freighter *Onondaga* ran aground on Watch Hill Reef in heavy fog, and sank in 50 feet of water. Two months later, the fishing steamer *George Hudson*, loaded with 1,000 barrels of menhaden, hit the reef in thick fog and sank. Fortunately, in both instances, all members of the crew were able to escape onto lifeboats before the vessels went down.

1933 The Event of the Schooner *Granville R. Bacon*

While most disasters are caused by storms, particularly during the winter season, the stranding of the three-masted *Granville R. Bacon* (home port Camden, Maine) was caused by a navigation error. On the evening of January 31, 1933, Captain *George Jones* mistook a white light of a street lamp off the beach at Weekapaug for the stern light of another vessel. Thinking he was following another vessel, the schooner grounded hard on the rocks along the shore with her cargo of coal.

The western beach patrol (surfman *Thomas Hartley*) from the Quonochontaug Life-Saving Station was alerted by the distress signals from the schooner and returned to the station where he roused the crew. Watch Hill Station was also notified and both crews arrived at the wreck site where Chief Boatswain *Arthur E. Larken* directed the rescue of the crew.

In an attempt to lighten her so she could be floated off, the crew and surfmen off loaded 240 bags of coal onto the beach, which disappeared by the next morning. After a number of attempts, she was given up as lost and her masts, rigging and other removable valuables were taken off.

The ultimate fate of the *Granville R. Bacon* was to be burned down to the waterline by the Watch Hill Fire Department in response to complaints by local residents. The grounded schooner had become a tourist attraction and the visitors were damaging private property to view the wreck.

5 Watch Hill

Schooner Granville R. Bacon stranded on Weekapaug Beach December 1933 *Colonial Research Center*

Chapter 6
Narragansett Pier Station USLLS #1
Coast Guard Station #54

The Narragansett Pier Station was the first station built in Rhode Island under the authorization of the newly established Life-Saving Service.

Records as to where the first station was located are vague. Official U.S. Coast Guard records indicate that the station was originally built in 1872 at 41° 25'59"N, 71° 27'04"W on the coast in the northern part of Narragansett Pier, and a second station was built in 1887 at 41° 25'45"N, 71° 27'20"W. These coordinates place the first station almost a mile north of the present (second) station.

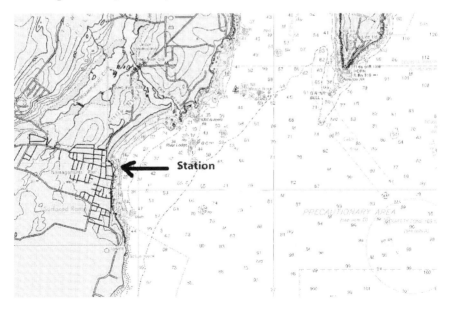

The second station building was unique. Unlike the gothic wooden designs of that era, the Narragansett Pier Station was constructed of stone. Almost foreboding, its appearance contrasted sharply with the somewhat frail looking wood structures of other stations being built at that time. This station's boat launching facilities were greatly improved in 1917. The station was formally decommissioned on July 15, 1937 and its equipment, including two 25-ft motorized surfboats and one pulling surfboat, was transferred to various stations in Massachusetts.

2011 images of the 1872 Narragansett Pier station house now converted into the Coast Guard House Restaurant at Narragansett. West view on the left, and south view with added decks and original stone anchor emblem on the right.   *Photos by author*

The Narragansett Pier Station is probably the best-known life-saving station in Rhode Island, not for its achievements or its life-saving endeavors, which were illustrious, but rather for its popular location. The Station is situated adjacent to Narragansett Beach, where thousands of people flock each summer. It is joined to the famous restored Coast Guard House with its twin towers and predominant arch straddling the state roadway Route A1A. The original Life-Saving Station building is the only one still standing of nine original life-saving stations in Rhode Island.

Centered in the middle of the stone complex with the highway on one side and the Bay on the other, it has been transformed into a popular and notable seaside restaurant called the Coast Guard House. Within its walls are artifacts and photographs recounting the life-saving station's use and remembrances of the crews.

Described as an "American tradition since 1945 the Coast Guard House has been synonymous with serving the freshest of seafood, delicious entrees, and the finest desserts in a casual, relaxed spectacular waterfront atmosphere." In 1979, the present owners completely renovated the structure making it into a year round dining facility and adding an outside deck which captivates patrons from the middle of April until the end of October. Known also as the Narragansett Pier Station, the restaurant has survived three major hurricanes that have decimated the property.

6 Narragansett Pier

Current view of the Narragansett Pier Station looking south with boat ramp
Photo Providence Public Library

Narragansett Pier crew harnessed to the beach apparatus cart
Photocopy from Coast Guard House Restaurant wall

Keepers *(from records of the USCG Historian's Office)*

"The early keepers were Benjamin Macomber (May 10, 1872 until he resigned on August 30, 1880), Albert Church

(September 4, 1880 until his death from "disease contracted in line of duty" on November 11, 1913), William Tucker (December 20, 1913 until incapacitated and retired on June 25, 1917), and Arthur L. Lanphere (reassigned from the Fishers Island Station on July 10, 1917, he was reassigned to the Maddeket Station on September 1, 1925). Next, Chief Petty Officers C.I. Williams appears as being in charge in 1927 (reassigned to the Maddeket Station in 1929) and then C.H. Collins (from the Point Judith Station in 1929)."

During the 1908 congressional hearings Keeper/Captain *Albert Church's* background and experience were entered into the records as follows:

"Capt. Albert Church, keeper of the Narragansett Pier Life-Saving Station, was born in the town of Charlestown, R. I. April 20, 1850. He entered the United States Life-Saving Service at the Narragansett Pier Station, under the command of Capt. Benjamin Macomber, November 15, 1875, as surfman No. 1. He was promoted to the keepership (succeeding Captain Macomber, who retired on age) September 10, 1880, a position he has since held with integrity and honor; during which time he has figured in many prominent wrecks in which many lives were saved, due mostly to his great courage, skill, and excellent judgment.

Before entering the Service, like many others that composed the life-saving crews in the early days of the Service, he was a shore fisherman. As a lifesaver he stands with the foremost in the art and skill of their profession.

He is in his fifty-eighth year, and being overtaken with infirmities of life and rheumatism produced by so many years of exposure in the discharge of his duties, is entitled to special recognition for faithful services."

Keepers were not the only ones singled out. One surfman, *Howard Browning*, in his striking dress uniform shows up in many photos and descriptions of the Narragansett Pier crew.

Photo of surfman Howard Browning of the Narragansett Pier Station
Photo USCG Archives

Selected Events Recorded in Annual LSS Reports
(Modified for Clarity by the Author)

1880 The Event of the Schooner *Peacedale*

On January 13, 1880 the schooner *Peacedale* of Newport under the command of *Captain Caswell* was sailing into Narragansett from South Amboy, New Jersey. Loaded with coal and with a crew of four men, the ship encountered gale force winds and heavy snow. Winds were from the northeast requiring her to tack up the Bay when she struck the rocks of Dickens Point near Bonnet Shores in the West Passage. The *Peacedale* came off the rocks without her rudder and had sprung a leak. Because of the snow, visibility was limited and the crew at Narragansett Station did not see the ship. At 7:00 PM the Station received a message that the *Peacedale* was sinking. The crew immediately launched their surfboat with head seas and in darkness rowed to the vessel stranded two miles north of their station. On arriving, they found the ship in sinking condition. Keeper *Albert Church* placed two surfmen aboard to help man the pumps, then returned to the station for a "relay" of men and to telegraph for the assistance of a tugboat. Returning to the vessel he placed two more men aboard and stood by until 2:00 AM when the tug arrived. The *Peacedale* was towed into the harbor with two surfmen still at the pumps and the vessel was saved. *Captain Caswell* published a report thanking the life-saving crew for their prompt and faithful service.

1877 The Event of the Schooner *Armenia*

On August 14, 1877 Keeper *Macomber* at the Narragansett Station sighted a ship grounded on Whale Rock. It was the schooner *Armenia* out of Tuckerton, New Jersey. Whale Rock, the smallest of the 30 islands in Narragansett Bay, is situated a third of a mile off the shore of Narragansett in the West Passage. As a result of heavy seas and high winds, the ship struck the rock around midnight, dragged her anchors and was totally destroyed. As a result of the collision, the captain of the *Armenia* broke his arm below the elbow and injured his hand severely. Keeper *Macomber* organized his crew to launch their surfboat from their station 1½ miles away. They rowed to the ship and had great difficulty protecting the surfboat from pounding against the rocks and the *Armenia*. The crew successfully saved the captain and the five crewmembers, along with their clothing. (Whale Rock did not have a lighthouse on it until 1882. In 1880 it was reported that over the previous six decades 56 lives had been lost in Whale Rock disasters.)

1882 The Event Concerning the Schooner *Janet S*

This event highlights the risks taken by surfmen and the personal injuries that occurred while they were trying to save a vessel. As noted by previous events, most all of Rhode Island's marine disasters took place in inclement weather. This event on April 21, 1882 was no different.

The *Janet S*, a British vessel with five men aboard out of Saint John, New Brunswick, had a load of lumber being delivered to Narragansett Pier. After unloading and leaving the pier she was caught by heavy seas and almost immediately driven on the rocks. The crew of the Narragansett Station came from less than a half mile away and boarded her in an attempt to float her off using her anchors and windlass. Heavy seas strained the load and the vessel lurched, knocking one surfman senseless on the deck with injuries and another thrown about receiving bad bruises. A third surfman was thrown overboard and almost drowned, but was rescued by other members of the life-saving crew. Unable to float the schooner, the vessel was stripped of its sails and rigging. It was pulled afloat the next day by a tug and towed to Providence for repairs.

1885 The Events of the Scows #15 and #17 and the Schooner *Lenonesa*

Both of these events took place on October 10, 1885 with heavy winds and seas. The tug *Gaynor*, unable to make headway, had to cast adrift her two scows #15 and #17. Both scows attempted to anchor, but soon began to drag. The station crew at Narragansett manipulated the beach apparatus opposite the two scows and attempted to fire a line that narrowly missed scow #17. Before another line could be rigged, the scow came close enough to shore so that the two men aboard could throw a line to the men on the beach. A hawser from the life-saving crew was then hauled aboard. On this line the crew made it to shore hand-over-hand. Shortly thereafter scow #15 fetched along side #17 and the three men aboard were able to transfer to #17 and come ashore by the same means.

Meanwhile, three miles north of the station the schooner *Lenonesa* was having difficulty in the gale. She stranded and was beginning to go to pieces. The life-saving crew finished up the rescue of the men from the two barges, gathered up their gear and rushed to the assistance of the schooner. They found her de-masted, with the sea raging over her decks and the crew barely able to maintain themselves on deck. The Lyle gun again was fired and within a half hour the crew of five was safely landed via the breeches buoy. By 2:00 PM in the afternoon the *Lenonesa* had broken into pieces. Both the saved crew and the surfmen were dangerously chilled. Through the kindness of *Mr. Horace L. Bloodgood*, who lived nearby, they were provided with food. At the same time, another schooner was reported to be in great danger and the surfboat and a tug were summoned. Luckily, before the arrival of either, the wind changed allowing the schooner to seek a place of safety.

1886 The Event Concerning *Miss Annie Lynch*

Saving lives was not limited to shipwrecks. The Narragansett Pier Station was adjacent to a popular bathing beach, which even during the late 1800s drew multitudes of bathers to the pristine sandy strip. Bathing was fashionable and enjoyable, but as always some bathers went in over their head and found themselves in trouble. Such was the case of *Miss Annie Lynch* of New York City who on August 12, 1886 narrowly escaped drowning thanks to the efforts of surfmen *Lewis Champlin* and *John Davis*. Apparently dead when rescued from the water, they applied "restoration" methods taught to the men of the service and succeeded in "bringing her around".

1890 The Events of the Schooners *A.H. Hurlburt* and *Bill Stowe*

Unfortunately, since the surfmen could not be in two places at once, one of these events resulted in the death of three men, including the captain of the vessel *A.H. Hurlburt*. This tragedy occurred at the same time the Narragansett Pier crew was saving seamen from another vessel, the *Bill Stowe*. The events took place the day after Christmas, December 26, 1890, in freezing weather when a very strong gale mixed with blinding snow blew into Narragansett Bay. Winds were clocked at 60 mph and seas were "rolling in ugly and dangerously".

The *A.H. Hurlburt* was a large three-masted schooner loaded with 400 tons of ice from Belfast, Maine bound for New York. She had passed the Vineyard Sound Lightship and set a new course for the Brenton Reef Lightship with the intent of rounding up into Newport Harbor for refuge. Due to the poor visibility, the captain did not sight the Brenton Reef Lightship and when they heard breakers dead ahead the crew of six tried to anchor. The attempt to anchor was not successful. The ship dragged and struck the rocks at Black Point about 2½ miles south of the Narragansett Pier Life-Saving Station. She pounded on the rocks and, being an old vessel, began to break up. Within twenty minutes of striking bottom the schooner had gone completely to pieces and the cargo of ice floated out of her hold.

The crew abandoned the wreckage of the ship and while attempting to swim ashore three men were drowned (captain, steward and a seaman) and three were pulled ashore by local residents. At the same time, the life-saving crew was saving the lives of the crew on the schooner *Bill Stowe* that was hard aground and also in the process of breaking up. This vessel was north of the station about three-quarters of a mile.

The *Bill Stowe,* also a three-masted schooner, was out of Boston and also destined for New York with a cargo of paving stones. She stranded about 1,000 feet off shore and pounded herself another 250 feet near to shore, breaking open her bottom and then going to pieces. The surfmen transported the beach apparatus cart to the site and shot a line to the deck that enabled the crew to secure it. With the assistance of local residents, including the ex-Governor of Rhode Island *William Sprague,* the six-man crew, one by one were carried safely ashore by the breeches buoy.

When this rescue was completed the crew hurriedly traveled south to Black Point to assist in the rescue of the *A.H. Hurlburt,* but it was too late. Both vessels were a total loss.

1892 The Event of the Schooner *Arvesta*

On March 2, 1892, during a heavy snowstorm with high winds and seas, the schooner *Arvesta* was found stranded. She had two feet of water in her hold and an attempt to get a steam pump aboard was unsuccessful. The crew of seven were taken off the vessel with their effects and housed at the station for two days. The vessel was left abandoned and subsequently went to pieces because of the pounding sea.

Miscellaneous Events

While saving lives of those aboard wrecked ships was the basic charter of the Life-Saving Service, often the surfmen were called upon to help with other matters. The incidents below are a few examples of the many non-shipwreck events that were recorded.

While returning to the Station at midnight on November 20, 1885, the north beach patrolman heard someone calling. Going toward the source of the sound he found a man lying on the beach unconscious with his face in the water. The surfman pulled the victim out, applied resuscitation methods on him and, when he had recovered sufficiently to stand up, walked the man home. The accident was due to intoxication, which made the man helpless and he fell into the water.

Another incident occurred on August 14, 1898 when the Narragansett Pier Station was called to ferry the lighthouse keeper and his district sergeant to the Whale Rock Lighthouse because of high seas. The lighthouse was situated six miles northeast of the Station and about a quarter of a mile off shore. The surfboat was much more stable and safer than the light dory normally used by the keepers at the Whale Rock Light. Incidentally, Whale Rock Light, along its Assistant Lighthouse Keeper *Earl Eberley*, was lost during the Great Hurricane of 1938.

6 Narragansett Pier

Chapter 7
Brenton Point Station
Coast Guard Station #53

The 1882 Authorization Act called for building a lifesaving station in the Newport area at either Beavertail Point on Conanicut Island, or in the vicinity of the city of Newport. The location selected was along the scenic south rocky shore of Newport Neck, less than one mile east of Brenton Point. More specifically, the site was at Price's Neck (41° 26'58"N, 71°20'10"W), a promontory of rock located off Ocean Drive and construction was completed in 1884.

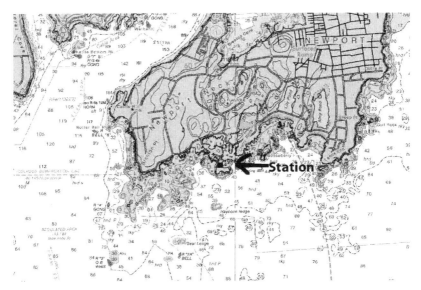

Price's Neck 2011   Photo by author

Paul Peltz, who had previously designed a number of lighthouses, designed the station. He completed plans for four identical life-saving stations, including the Brenton Point Station. The other three stations were located in New Jersey at Atlantic City, Bayhead, and Deal. The unusual building design included a distinctive steeple tower unlike any of the other life-saving stations built.

Brenton Point Station on Price's Neck. The boat house was located under the roof on the left side of the building. Post Card, Providence Public Library

In 1912 a new boathouse and surfboat launch way were constructed alongside the station building. The station doors and launching area were designed and built on a sheltered beach that afforded favorable launching into calm water rather than through surf.

The station location was also the site of a U.S. Navy radio compass station. In the 1920s, 25 radio direction finding stations were established from Bar Harbor, Maine to Key West, Florida to provide a point of bearing for vessels equipped with radio directional finding (RDF) equipment. The radio compass stations emitted a coded radio signal with a range out to 150 miles from shore. Since radio signals followed the curvature of the earth, navigators were warned to use only gnomonic projection charts, and not Mercator charts which would not accurately project the radio signals. By 1930 these radio stations were operated and maintained by the U.S. Coast Guard.

The life-saving station at Price's Point was totally destroyed by the Great Hurricane of 1938. In 1941, the Brenton Point Station was re-located to Castle Hill Cove on the East Passage of Narragansett Bay. Historian *Tim Dring* writes on the effect of 1938 hurricane:

> *"This station and its rescue boats/equipment were heavily damaged in the famous 1938 Hurricane, as described in the station logbook entry of 21 September 1938. In terms of structures, the main station house was heavily damaged such that continued operations and berthing in this building were no longer safe or practical. The detached boathouse and marine railway were destroyed, along with the detached garage. In the boathouse, and destroyed along*

with it, were the station's beach apparatus and carts, as well as Race Point type pulling surfboat No. 4120 and dory No. 4603. Ripped from its mooring and swept ashore in the storm surge was the station's 36 ft. Type HR (R=revised) motor lifeboat No. 2052. Although later refloated, it was sufficiently damaged that a replacement motor lifeboat (newer 36 ft. 8 in. Type TRS motor lifeboat No. 5192/CG36453) was secured."

The hurricane caused extensive losses and damage to the station, including its detached boathouse. All of its equipment, beach apparatus, carts, surfboats, supplies, spare parts, fuel, and marine launching railway were lost. The station's 38-ft. cabin picket boat, No. 2393/CG38309, was in Newport Harbor at the time of the storm, where it safely rode out the hurricane and storm surge. The hurricane of 1938 was so devastating that the U.S. Congress authorized personal payment of losses experienced by Coast Guard personnel at Price's Neck. Claims were submitted and paid to M.M. *Charles Adamson* ($90.25), Surfman *Willi Bastareche* ($541.45), Surfman *George Gautreau* ($52.00), Chief Boatswain Mate *George Lewis* ($93.00), Surfman *Manuel Macedo* ($61.65), Surfman *Leonard McCarthy* ($81.00), Boatswain Mate *Ralph Small* ($54.50), Surfman *Coulter Tillet* ($26.00) and M.M. *George Williams* ($52.50).

Following the disaster, station personnel response assistance was still needed. Station operations resumed immediately with the crew berthed at the Seaman's Church Institute in downtown Newport and on the picket boat berthed at Government Wharf in Newport Harbor. This was the situation until late 1941 when the replacement station was completed at Castle Hill. During World War II (1942), an anti-aircraft training station was established at the original Price's Neck site. The Price's Neck property was abandoned in 1946. Today, Price's Neck is occupied by exclusive estates and homes. The original road leading to the station site is no longer public, and the location of the original station is further restricted by an electronic security gate limiting access to the private property.

Keepers *(from records of the USCG Historian's Office)*

The early keepers at Price's Neck were *Albert C. Gould* (appointed October 30, 1884 and resigned March 20, 1887), *Chauncey C. Kenyon* (March 26, 1887 until his retirement with thirty years service on October 15, 1920), *Frank E. Allison* (reassigned from the Coskata Station on May 3, 1921 and reassigned as Assistant to the Superintendent of the Third District in Bay Shore New York on July 17, 1922), *Albert Rohdin* (reassigned from the Coskata Station on August 3, 1922, he was reassigned to the Quonochontaug Station on March 15, 1926), and *George W. Streeter* (from the Quonochontaug Station on March 15, 1926 and reassigned to the New Shoreham Station on February 21, 1928). Next came Chief Petty Officer *S.E. Littlefield*, who went to the New Shoreham Station. The last keeper at Price's Neck was Chief Boatswain Mate *George Lewis*.

The first crew at the Brenton Point Station, in addition to Keeper *Albert Gould*, was *Ray. S. Scott, George Calvert, Joseph Casey, Charles S. Esleeck, Lelant H. Groff* and *William H. Spooner*.

7 Brenton Point

In 1908 Keeper *Chauncey Kenyon* and Surfman *Joseph Carey* were singled out during congressional hearings in Washington as examples of exemplary service:

"Capt. C.C. Kenyon was born at Point Judith, R.I. January 30, 1859. He entered the United States Life-Saving Service as a surfman November 15, 1877, succeeding his father, who was one of the original crew at that station. His elegant qualifications were recognized by the district officers of the Service, when he was promoted to the keepership of the Brenton Point Station in April 11, 1887 (succeeding Capt. A.G. Gould, resigned), a position he now holds.

Since connected with the service he has cooperated in many successful rescues both at Point Judith and his own station.

May 4, 1904, during a fire at the Brenton Point Station, he performed a very creditable and heroic act in taking the principle part in putting out a fire that threatened to destroy the station and whole outfit, thereby saving the station and apparatus which could not be replaced for more than $20,000. In this brave act he suffered great torture by being burned beyond recognition, and so frightfully that when seen by his wife she was so terribly shocked she gave premature birth to a child, and her death soon followed, leaving two small children that are being cared for at considerable expense to him. A detailed report of the fire made on May 5, 1904, by the district superintendent, accompanied by photographs showing the frightful manner in which he was burned, is attached.

He also, with his crew, rendered timely and valuable service at the time the Davis stable was burned, and they are credited with saving the Davis mansion in which Davis was ill at the time.

Captain Kenyon has served the Service faithfully both as surfman and keeper for the past thirty years. He is 48 years of age, and though badly scarred and disfigured about the hands, neck, and face from his heroic work, is yet agile, and still is a person whose noble work and brave deeds of the past are worthy of special recognition.

Surfman Joseph Casey was born November 17, 1813, and has always lived and fished about Newport, R.I.

He entered the Life-Saving Service as Surfman No. 7 of the Brenton Point crew December 1, 1884. Resigned April 1, 1887, to attend to important business. Reentered the Service the next active season and resigned again August 1, 1898. He reentered the Service August 1, 1899, and owing to his good qualifications was made No. 1 of the crew, a position he now holds.

He has figured in all of the wrecks having occurred within the jurisdiction of that station, and was one of the principals in fighting the fire at that station, and also took an active part at the fire on the Davis estate at the time the stable was burned and the Davis mansion saved by the valuable services of the Brenton Point life-saving crew. He is 44 years of age and the main support of two or three sisters."

The U.S. Coast Guard Castle Hill Station (#34) is the present central search and rescue operation in Narragansett Bay. The new station, completed in 1941, includes the navigation flashing red Castle Hill Light, a large Roosevelt style station house with a communications center, a boat basin with a two-bay boat house, marine railway and docks at Castle Hill Cove down the hill to the west of station. The cove is shared with The Inn at Castle Hill, a popular restaurant and inn located on the property adjacent to the Castle Hill Lighthouse and overlooking the East Passage of Narragansett Bay.

Present Castle Hill Station constructed 1941 at Castle Hill Cove
Photo by author

Selected Events Recorded in Annual LSS Reports (Modified for Clarity by the Author)

1892 The Event of the Schooner *Promised Safety*

As already noted, life-saving was only part of the job; the other part was saving vessels by any and every means available. When a vessel grounded unintentionally the station crews did whatever was necessary to save the ship and crew. In November 1892 the schooner *Promised Safety* was in danger of foundering during a gale and was saved by the Brenton Station crew.

Promised Safety, a 50-ton fishing vessel from New Bedford, was anchored off Sachuest Point during a gale and broke away from her moorings as her ground tackle gave way. Luckily, she by-passed rocks on either side and was firmly beached at high tide. The Brenton Station crew with the assistance of a local farmer, *Mr. Herman Peckham,* and three of his hands worked all afternoon and well into the evening. After supper at the house of Mr. *Peckham,* they all returned at 2:00 AM to continue digging into the next morning. After burying a heavy log at low water as a rigging anchor and laying out tackle to *Promised Safety,* they worked her out with pries from the sand bed and turned her head to the sea. Keeper *Chauncey C. Kenyon* and crew laid out three anchors and cables and after two attempts, which took up the rest of the day, *Promised Safety* finally floated off at high water. The life-saving crew with its own boat managed to move *Promised Safety* out of the shoals nearly to Cormorant Rock. It was near dark when she then headed up the Sakonnet River.

1885 The Event of the Schooner *Eva L. Leonard*

On the evening of January 13, 1885 the schooner *Eva L. Leonard* ran ashore 2¾ miles from the station. It was freezing cold and snowing, and no doubt poor visibility contributed to the stranding. The captain had difficulty restraining two crewmen from abandoning the vessel in the ship's yawl. The timely arrival of the life-saving station crew prevented the disaster from turning deadly. With the help of four local residents the breeches buoy apparatus was deployed and the four men on board the *Leonard* were safely landed on the

7 Brenton Point

beach. The rescued crew was taken care of at a nearby house. The mate's hand was frozen and treated with remedies from the station's medicine chest. The crew received dry clothing from the Station. The following day the vessel was stripped and the crew's effects were saved.

1886 The Event of the Schooner *Mattie D*

When winter cold and snow are combined with a gale, life-saving incidents are stressful for both the crews on board stricken vessels and those from the life-saving stations. Such was the case of the schooner *Mattie D* on January 9, 1886. The ship was loaded with a cargo of salt from the West Indies and heading to Portsmouth, New Hampshire. Late in the afternoon the crew of Brenton (Price's Neck) Station sighted the schooner under "bare poles", her sails torn away, trying to steer to Newport Harbor. The westerly winds were driving her leeward toward the rocky shore south of Castle Hill. Keeper *Albert Gould* mobilized his surfmen to pack up the beach apparatus and began a trek along the coastline over snow drifts to a point where he thought the *Mattie D* would hit the rocks. Progress was slow with men hauling the cart, and the heavy apparatus getting stuck in the snowdrifts. Keeper *Gould* commandeered a team of horses from farmer *Jonathan Kenny*, allowing the lifesavers to move more quickly toward the anticipated grounding site. Meanwhile, the *Mattie D* had raised part of her torn mainsail and her jib topsail. In short order the jib topsail burst apart in shreds and the schooner's last chance to avoid the rocks was gone. She came aground at Raggard Point. *Gould* and his crew arrived five minutes later, but because the area was fissured with rock crevices they could not get closer than 150 yards. Water was now breaking over the *Mattie D's* deck from stern to bow while she was wallowing back and forth on the rocks. Keeper *Gould* worked himself over the rocks and got close enough to get a messenger line over the vessel's jib boom from which they hauled in a hawser and rigged the breeches buoy fast. The luckless captain of the schooner tried to leap from the vessel onto the rocks and fell into the sea between two crevices. He would have been washed out to sea by the next wave if not for Keeper *Gould's* prompt action in grabbing the captain's arm and pulling him to safety. The remaining five members of the crew were safely brought ashore one by one using the breeches buoy. All the sailors had frostbite and rather than transporting them to the station two miles away, *Gould* secured housing and immediate care for them at the house of *Mr. Martland* who lived nearby. *Gould* went back to the station to secure clothes from his own wardrobe and that of the station's crew and returned to *Martland's* house so that the crew of the *Mattie D* could change into dry clothes. Two hours after the rescue the *Mattie D* had completely broken up into pieces.

1887 The Event of the Schooner *Dove*

During the day watch at 8:00 AM of April 28, 1887, the schooner *Dove* while on route to New Bedford anchored dangerously near some rocks. Surfman from the station at once put off in their surfboat to help her get underway, but the vessel mis-stayed and went on the reef. The life-saving crew, with help of some fisherman, succeeded in getting her clear, but the ship was leaking with the loss of her rudder. The vessel struck the rocks and her captain was thrown overboard. Fortunately, the life-saving crew rescued him.

7 Brenton Point

1896 The Event of the Schooner *Water Witch*

The *Water Witch* went aground on March 19, 1896 during a heavy gale, but was not seen by the watch since she stranded nine miles east of the station. Word was not received until the following morning that assistance was needed. With the gale and high seas still raging the keeper procured a team of horses and loaded the beach apparatus knowing that it would be impossible to launch the surfboat into the seas and row nine miles. When they reached the spot, they found the vessel broken up with the ship's crew having landed in their own boat and being cared for by a nearby resident, *Mr. H.F. Peckman*. Using a team owned by him, the crew of seven were taken to the life-saving station where they were given clothing from the supply of the Women's National Relief Association. The crew was transported to Boston two days later.

1896 The Event of the Schooner *Helen F. Whittin*

On September 9, 1896, during a heavy gale with sixteen men aboard, the sails of the schooner *Helen F. Whittin* were split and, uncontrolled, she was driven up on the rocks 150 ft off the shore of Pine Tree Point (just below Castle Hill, about 2½ miles north northwest of the station). The vessel was out of Gloucester, Massachusetts and was loaded with mackerel recently caught off of Sakonnet. This was one of the worse gales in years and the ship made an unsuccessful attempt to reach Newport Harbor. Losing her headsails, she tried to drop two anchors, but neither held. The floundering ship was seen by the patrol who immediately secured two teams of horses, loaded the beach apparatus and the station's surfboat, and then made their way abreast of the vessel.

On the first attempt the shot line was laid aboard the *Whittin*, the whip with hawser sent off and the beach gear set up. Nine of the ship's crew lowered the vessel's yawl and by means of the rigged hawser were brought safely ashore. The vessel was rolling heavily in the surf, requiring the tackles to be frequently readjusted. It was with great difficulty that the remaining seven crewmembers were brought ashore by the breeches buoy. The crew was housed at the station for two days and when the weather had subsided the surfmen assisted in getting some of the cargo aboard off loaded. Eight days later, after removing 23 tons of ballast, wreckers succeeded in floating her off and towed the schooner to Newport for repairs.

1898 The Event of the Dories Belonging to the Schooner *Actress*

This report does not indicate how six dories belonging to a sunken schooner, the *Actress*, were discovered on August 26, 1898, 10 miles out to sea from the station at Price's Neck. The dories were well below the horizon and not within visible range of the station. It is assumed that the station surfboat at that time did not have a motor, since a later report in 1909 discusses the "new station power life boat named Ida Lewis".

> *"Discovered about 10 miles S by E of the station, lifesavers went out to them by surfboat and found they contained the crew of the American fishing schooner the Actress, who had sprung a leak 29 miles S by E of Brenton Point, and they had barely time to get into the dories before she sank. The keeper directed four of the dories to pull for the station, then he went on with the surfboat to the two offshore dories*

which contained one man each. As the men pulling these two dories were tired out, the surfboat took them in tow and returned to the station. All were furnished with supper and given shoes and socks from the supply of the Women's National Relief Association and later supplied with transportation to Boston. The dories were hauled up on the beach until disposed of by the owner."

1905 The Event of the Schooner *George & Albert*

A somewhat strange occurrence took place on April 7, 1905 when the crew of the Price's Neck Station was called about a two-masted schooner, the *George & Albert*, that had sunk near Cormorant Rock with people still hanging in the rigging. The 121-ton vessel was on route from New Bedford, Massachusetts to New York City and was sighted in distress by several people.

Cormorant Rock sits four miles east of the Price's Neck Life-Saving Station and over a half mile south of Sachuest Point at the mouth of the Sakonnet River. Unable to see over the terrain to the east, Captain *Kenyon* of the station trudged to the nearby cliffs, viewed the wreck and saw men in the rigging. With a boiling sea running around the wreck, he arranged for a tugboat to pick him up with his crew and the station's surfboat from the quiet waters of the station's launching ramp and re-launch them near Cormorant Rock.

However, neither the vessel nor its crew could be found and it was not until the day after that a report was made that the schooner's captain, his wife and three crew members had made off in a small boat and landed safely at Sakonnet.

1909 The Event of the Collier *Nero*

This event was the result of heavy fog on July 1, 1909. The Navy collier, *Nero,* departing Newport Harbor on route to Boston, went hard aground on Brenton Reef with a civilian crew of 30 men aboard. At the time, the life-saving station at Price's Neck was on their summer schedule and only the Keeper *John Kenyon* was on duty. He observed the vessel on the reef after the fog had lifted.

On the reef, the collier's hull was fractured and she was taking on water. The steam-operated pumps were manned and they began pumping water out of the hull. Keeper *Kenyon* rounded up a volunteer crew to man the surfboat to help. Two days later strong winds and sea had built up and the beach apparatus was made ready to take off her crew, but it was not necessary. The *Nero* remained stuck on the reef for a month. The life-saving crew removed seven boilers by surfboat and pumping compressed air to replace the water finally floated the Nero free and enlisting the aid of six Navy tugs to pull the vessel off the reef.

1913 The Event of the Schooner *Wm. A. Grozier*

This event demonstrated the benefit of the powered life boat added to all the life-saving stations in 1909. The powered life boat provided greater endurance and strength for pulling large vessels off rocks, compared to the ability of oarsmen.

On May 19, 1913 at about 6:00 AM, the 116-ton schooner *Wm. A. Grozier* bound for New Bedford from Newport was swept ashore by the tide 2½ miles west by north of the Brenton Point Station. When the life-saving crew arrived alongside with their power lifeboat, they found the vessel on the inside of Butter Ball Rock with two launches standing by, one with a line tangled in her propeller. A gale was blowing on shore and it was out of the question for either of the launches to assist the schooner. The keeper therefore went ashore and sent messages by wireless to the cutter *Acushnet* and to a boat towing company.

The schooner was in an extremely dangerous situation, made doubly so by the fact the tide was falling. She was pounding heavily on her stern and Wash Ball Rock was within 20 ft of her bow, ready to crush her should her anchors fail to hold. In his report the keeper says:

> *"I never believed we could get her out of the place and keep her off the shore to leeward. We put a line on the port bow, the schooner crew hoisted sail and I got the boat in position and started ahead full speed. We dragged her clear of everything and well across the bay and hauled her around on the port tack. Then I went ahead and piloted her into the harbor. She was leaking quite bad. Her crew had been pumping for some 20 hours before she reached New Bedford and they were all exhausted. So we stayed with them all night and pumped, watch and watch. In the morning we helped put on the marine railway the launch that had got the line around her propeller while trying to assist the schooner*

> *People who saw us take the vessel off the rocks said it was one of the finest things they ever witnessed. They had no idea we could pull her away. We had our boat running nine hours and she was on the move the moment we opened her up. I had her wide open for over an hour. For a while we needed all the power she had."*

1924 The Event of the Steamship *Llewellyn Howland*

While this event took place after the Life-Saving Service was merged into the U.S. Coast Guard, the dramatic account of the vessel's misfortune warrants inclusion with Brenton Station history.

On April 21, 1924, the *Llewellyn Howland,* a 283-ft bulk oil transport ship, departed from Fall River for Portland, Maine. She stranded on Seal Ledge southwest of Brenton Reef and immediately ruptured her tanks. The cause was never fully understood, other than she was off course. The Coast Guard launched a power lifeboat and the crew was safely removed from the wreck. Three days later, while still on the rocks, the vessel was officially designated as abandoned, and left to government agencies to take action. It was decided to set her on fire and burn off the remaining oil to protect the nearby beaches from pollution. The fire continued for over 130 hours, and the remaining oil in her underwater hull was dispersed with two charges of TNT.

1928 The Event of the Barge *Harry Keeler*

On January 27, 1928, an unusually strong winter gale ripped through Narragansett Bay leaving wreckage and havoc in its wake. There was widespread damage in Newport, including the destruction of the Bailey's Beach roller coaster. Buildings, small boats and barges were catastrophes. The storm moved slowly, thereby intensifying damage along the beaches.

The barge *Harry Keeler* dragged her anchors and came ashore on the rocks near the Navy Training Base. Aboard were the captain, his wife and their dog. The lifesavers from Price's Neck, under the command of Captain *George Streeter,* attempted an unsuccessful rescue by boat and then reverted to rigging the beach apparatus. The Lyle gun was successfully fired, the line broached over the barge and then tied fast to the barge by the captain on board. The woman was first to be swung over the side in the breeches buoy and began the perilous trip to safety hauled in by the surfmen.

Rescue of the captain from the wreck of the Harry Keeler 1928
Photo J. Jenny files

All, however, did not go well. Part way to shore the hawser line slackened, the rope dropped into the water, dragged and then caught something under water. With less tension on the line, the woman was inadvertently submerged under water. Rescuers saw the line entangled in wreckage from the barge and with the help of standby volunteers pulled on the breeches buoy hawser that was tangled with wreckage. The heavy load of barge timbers and the woman were dragged ashore where they found the woman barely conscious. The lines were cleared and the second trip to rescue the captain was successful. The woman survived, but not the dog; and the barge was a total loss.

7 Brenton Point

Chapter 8
Point Judith Station USLLS #2
Coast Guard Station #55

Point Judith Station sits on the picturesque spit of rock and beach called Point Judith. Its biblical connotation (Jude) may have influenced the naming of the two nearby villages of Galilee and Jerusalem. Point Judith, a popular public summer destination, was also an established fishing port. In 1914 a V-shaped two-mile long breakwater was constructed on its western shore, protecting the entrance into Point Judith Pond.

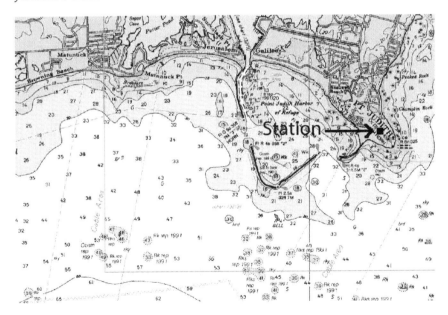

Within a distance of a few hundred yards of the extreme southeast end of the point, a light station, life-saving station and a radio communications station existed.

Point Judith

The first life-saving station, one of the earliest established by the Service, was built in 1876 and was operational on June 15 of the same year. By November it was up for full service. The property had been purchased the previous year and was located about an eighth of a mile north of Point Judith on the northwest side of the Point. According to an 1877 New York Times article written by a reporter accompanying inspectors to the station:

> *"Point Judith is one of the most barren and uninhabited places on the coast at least 10 miles from any civilization. The neighboring farmers rake out sea weed and leave it to decay on the beach for manure and the sickening smell floats for miles into the interior giving the whole of that part of the state the odor of an apothecary's store room."*

Over the life of the station, three different building types were used. Francis W. Chandler designed the 1876 structure. It was one of 20 similar stations called an 1875 Type that was constructed both on the Atlantic seaboard and in the Great Lakes. Somewhat gothic in style with elaborate decorative wood bracketing, the living quarters were above the boathouse. The building included a cupola lookout attached to the top of the roof, and included a tall flagstaff. The large boathouse door had a ramp allowing the boat cradle to be wheeled out of the building.

For unknown reasons, eleven years later (1888) a new building was built. This second station was a Bibb Type 2, one of 22 similar station structures built during the period 1887-1891. In addition to living quarters, it had an attached boathouse, a large front porch, and a copula on the roof for use as the lookout. The boathouse also garaged the station's beach cart and life-saving equipment. A similar structure without the porch was built at the same time on Block Island as the New Shoreham Station.

Point Judith Life-Saving Station with a Bibb Type 2 building (right) built in 1888 with the 1875 Type building on the left. Photo RI News Co.

The Coast Guard lists the coordinates of the station as 41° 21'40"N, 71° 29'00"W.

The geographic importance of Point Judith cannot be understated. As a sandy point of land jutting into sea, it separates Rhode Island Sound from Block Island Sound; and has contributed much to the history of Rhode Island. Its location was crucial for shipping cargo destined for Newport, Fall River and Providence. For vessels continuing into Long Island Sound or easterly along the southern reaches of Cape Cod, the Elizabeth Islands, Martha's Vineyard and Nantucket or around the Cape to Boston and beyond, Point Judith was the navigation "way point" or the "fix" used by navigators to confirm a ship's position and set the next compass course. Thousands of vessels in astounding numbers passed the Point each year. Despite the presence of the lighthouse, frequent wrecks occurred in the vicinity. In 1855 alone, 16 vessels were wrecked or stranded near Point Judith. Shipping traffic past Point Judith remained heavy throughout the 19th century.

Lighthouse keepers were required by the U.S. Lighthouse Board to log every sighted vessel by time, type and direction, plus noting the weather conditions at the time of sighting. During the one-year period from June 1, 1871 to June 1, 1872, near the height of America's maritime coastal commerce era, *Joseph Whaley*, the lighthouse keeper at Point Judith, and his assistant reported that "4,444 steamers, 2,183 sloops, 29,757 schooners, 728 brigs, 122 barks and 23 other ships" passed by the Point Judith light, a total of over 37,000 vessels. Almost 40 years later (1907), as railroads expanded and became the nation's primary conveyance of goods, 22,860 vessels were counted passing the lighthouse in daylight hours. This number was four times greater than the ship traffic entering New York Harbor. Despite the lighthouse, frequent wrecks continued in the vicinity.

Chapter 1 of this book mentions Rhode Island's worse maritime disaster, the collision and sinking of the steamer *Larchmont* off Watch Hill. Hundreds died and debris washed ashore all along Rhode Island's south shore, Block Island and Point Judith. Artifacts are few and far between. One relic is found hanging on a wall in a popular seafood restaurant near Point Judith, George's of Galilee.

A life preserver from the Larchmont on display at George's of Galilee restaurant near Point Judith, RI.

Photo by author

The current Point Judith Coast Guard Station was built in 1937 on the grounds of the Point Judith Light, established in 1809 and the third oldest lighthouse in Rhode Island. The station sits at the extreme southern end of the Point. In addition to the lighthouse and its fog signal, it serves as a Search and Rescue station covering part of Narragansett Bay, and both Rhode Island and Block Island Sounds. Each year Point Judith Station still responds to hundreds of rescue cases a year.

The Massie Radio Station

In 1907 *Walter Wentworth Massie,* who was a contemporary of *Guglielmo Marconi,* built a radio station on Point Judith. This station was one of the first applications of marine telegraph communications from shore. The station mainly served passenger steamboats traveling between New York City and New England using a "spark-gap" transmitter operating on 350 kHz. It was situated inside of the dune where the eastern end of the present breakwater joins the beach. A small cupola on top of the building was used as a lookout for identifying passing ships. By a fortuitous combination of circumstances, the entire abandoned Point Judith *Massie* radio station building was moved from its site in 1983 to the New England Wireless and Steam Museum in East Greenwich. The 1907 building is unaltered and still contains its original radio equipment in working order, which is demonstrated to visitors at the museum from time to time by licensed amateur radio operators.

The Massie Spark Gap Radio Station at Point Judith before being moved to the New England Wireless and Steam Museum in East Greenwich, RI
Photo courtesy of NEWSM

Keepers *(from records of the USCG Historian's Office)*

Eight keepers were assigned to the Point Judith Life-Saving Station over its 62 years of operation.

> "*The first appointed keeper was a fisherman, Joseph N. Griffin, who was appointed at the age of 33 on September 14, 1876; he was removed on February 18, 1878. The next keeper was Daniel Billington, who was appointed effective February 11, 1878; the date of the end of his tenure was*

unrecorded. The next keeper was Herbert M. Knowles, who was appointed from one of the crew at the age of 24 on December 5, 1878 (see below). Next came Asa Church (October 3, 1889 until his resignation due to physical reasons on May 15, 1905), and Amos P. Tefft (April 25, 1905 until his reassignment to the Sandy Point Station on June 24, 1922). He was followed by Chief Petty Officer C. H. Collins, who is listed in 1927 and shown going to the Narragansett Pier Station in 1929. Next appears Adolph A. Rohdin, from the Cuttyhunk Station on August 25, 1928, who served until December 2, 1935 when he was reassigned to the Office of the Third District. The last commanding officer listed before World War II was Arthur E. Larkin, who arrived on July 15, 1937 from the Quonochontaug Station."

Keeper Herbert M. Knowles

The *Knowles* family maintained a farm on Point Judith and in 1809 sold a parcel from the property for $300 to the U.S. government to build a lighthouse there. The lighthouse was swept off its foundation during the September 23 Great Gale of 1815. The elder *Knowles*, a son and four workmen drowned trying to save boats.

Herbert M. Knowles, a descendant of the family had joined the Life-Saving Service as a surfman at Point Judith Station. He was a young man, 24 years of age, when he was picked out of the surfmen crew and appointed keeper of the station on December 5, 1878. He remained as keeper until 1889 and because of his extraordinary accomplishments, and management capabilities he was recognized by the Washington, D.C. Superintendent of the Life-Saving Service

Sumner Kimball. Kimball appointed *Knowles* the Assistant District Superintendent of the Third District, and later as the District Superintendent. *Knowles* served in this capacity from an office in Wakefield. He was also selected to serve on the prestigious Apparatus Evaluation Committee. It is not known when he left the service. It is worthy to relate two other major events he was involved with while he was keeper at Point Judith Station, both of which resulted in exemplary letters of commendation from those he helped.

Selected Events Recorded in Annual LSS Reports (Modified for Clarity by the Author)

Saving lives sounds dramatic and the men at Point Judith did indeed save many. However, their duties encompassed many activities, and even when lives were not necessarily in jeopardy, their actions in related marine events earned the respect of those who they helped. Below are sample excerpts from Life-Saving Service Reports attesting to some of those other deeds. Although simple in statement, the reader can envision the complications and energies expended to help others.

1869 The Event of the Brig *Meteor*

> *"The Brig Meteor went aground. Herbert Whaley (also a light keeper) got the crew and a single passenger ashore and hosted them in the station, but then threw them out when he found they had a contagious sickness on board."*

1883 The Event of the Sloop *Jennie*

In May 1883, the sloop *Jennie* went aground in dense fog off the station. With two feet of water in her hold, the crew of two men, who were drenched, were brought to the station in need of dry clothing and food. The life-saving station crew and the sloop's crew returned to the vessel and unloaded 9,000 bricks to lighten load, ran out two anchors, pumped her out and re-floated the vessel. The two crewmembers were then taken care of for two more days.

1885 The Event of the schooner *Almon Bacon*

Shortly before 2:00 PM on November 5, 1885 during a rough sea, the crew of Point Judith Station observed a schooner under reduced sails two miles to the east of the station flying a distress signal. Before they had gone half way to the vessel, it sank with nothing other than her topmasts showing. The schooner's five-man crew had launched their yawl as the vessel sank. The surfboat crew took them in tow to the station where they were fed and housed. She was the *Almon Bacon* out of New York headed for Providence with a cargo of 150 tons of pig iron and 27 tons of logwood. She had sprung a leak off New London and when near Point Judith a planking burst and she floundered almost immediately in 12 fathoms of water. The following day Keeper *Knowles* conveyed the ship's crew in his wagon to Wakefield, procured passes for them to proceed to Providence by rail, in addition to furnishing them with funds. For two weeks the station crew maintained a beacon light on the vessel until she finally disappeared and was classified as a total loss.

1885 The Event of Schooners *Mott Haven* and *Willie De Wolf*

"It was Christmas day December 25, 1885 in the midst of a ferocious gale when the crew of the Point Judith surfboat

made a most perilous trip several miles offshore to two wrecked vessels. The event started at 7:30 in the morning when Keeper Knowles discovered a schooner capsized and waterlogged south of the station. A mile further out, sticking out of the water were the masts of another vessel. Knowles with his telescope saw people clinging to both vessels and judged correctly that the vessels had collided. The life-saving crew was called out and launched the surfboat loaded with spare clothing, provisions and medical supplies. By 9:00 they had reached the nearest schooner which was almost submerged with her cargo of lumber and laths floating away. She was held by her anchors that the crew had let go after they were run into and before she capsized. Her small boat was gone and there was no sign of life. Knowles and his crew then headed for the second sunken vessel, again finding no one aboard. By this time the wind had increased and utmost care was needed to prevent the surfboat from swamping or capsizing. Attempts to return to Point Judith were unsuccessful. The seas prevented any headway and rowing was futile. The station was now miles to windward and impossible to reach. The only hope was to run with the wind and seas to Block Island eight to ten miles away. It was a "perilous undertaking" and two hours later they reached the New Shoreham Station where they were welcomed by both the life-saving crew and the crew of the sunken schooner Mott Haven of Calais, Maine. The Mott Haven was on her way from New York to Calais with a cargo of coal. It was learned that she had been run down and sunk by the schooner Willie De Wolf, coincidently also from Calais and bound for New York. The Mott Haven crew did not know what became of the De Wolf's crew. The gale continued to build with winds estimated to be sixty to seventy miles per hour. The following morning the De Wolf with parted cables came ashore on the north end of the island and broke up into a complete wreck. Both the New Shoreham and Point Judith life-saving crews attempted to salvage parts of her cargo, but their efforts were of no use. Meanwhile, back on the mainland there were great fears that the Point Judith crew was lost. Telegraph communications were out of order to Block Island to contact the crew at New Shoreham. The Assistant Superintendent of the district, Captain John Waters of Newport, charted a small ten-ton vessel Mystery and in gale force winds set out in search of missing surfboat. Sighting nothing, he continued to Block Island arriving around 10:00 AM after a very rough passage. Happy to see the life station crew alive, he told them the survivors of the De Wolf were picked up by a passing vessel and they had landed in Newport. Captain Waters was anxious to get the word back that the crew of Point Judith Station were safe and to get them back to station. He chartered another slightly larger schooner, the Arabella, took the surfboat in tow and headed as best they could north. The Arabella almost immediately parted her head stay and was crippled in the water. Repairs were made and although she was knocked on beam-ends several times, the vessel covered with ice, reached Newport about 6:00 PM."

The incredible part of this story is that not a single life was lost. The determination of the men overcame the harshness of a cold winter gale, ice-covered ships, cold hands on oars and dangerous passages in an open surfboat. It was a miracle that the crews survived sinking and were able to get themselves ashore. The incident fortifies the stories of heroic seafaring men who placed their lives at risk for others; and after experiencing physical and mental ordeals, go back to their station ready to face dangers again and again.

1886 The Event of the Schooner *Allen Green*

On January 9, 1886 the severest storm of the season, reportedly blowing hurricane strength accompanied with snow squalls, was raging along the lower coast of Block Island Sound. The three-masted schooner *Allen Green* of Providence was sailing from Boston to Baltimore in ballast and was unable to sustain the sea and wind. The ship lost the ability to maneuver and was driven ashore a mile west of the Point Judith Station near Galilee (the breakwater had not yet been constructed). She was discovered by the beach patrol of Point Judith Station in the early afternoon. The crew, under the direction of Keeper *Knowles*, manned the apparatus beach cart and tried unsuccessfully to trudge through snow banks. A team of horses was obtained and with the assistance of the Point Judith Lighthouse keeper, *Henry A. Whaley*, and a man named *Howard Donahue* they succeeded in getting abreast of the vessel in a half hour. This was accomplished by "downright hard work, shoveling, removing fences and stone walls." The *Allen Green* lay 500 ft from shore awash in sea and foam. The crew had climbed into the rigging to save themselves. Keeper *Knowles* aligned the Lyle gun and the first shot lodged forward over the jib boom. The vessel's crew was half frozen and their clothing covered with ice; they were unable to descend to the deck and the line slipped into the sea. Pulling the frozen line back and attempting to re-flake it was futile. A second shot with the weakened brittle line snapped close to the gun. On the third try, the line lodged on a stay between the fore and main mast out of reach of the crew. After some vigorous shaking, a bight of the line was caught and the crew hauled in the "whip" and then the hawser. The breeches buoy was rigged thanks to the mate of the schooner who himself had been saved on three previous occasions by a breeches buoy. The seven crewmen of the *Allen Green* were drawn ashore and taken to the station. Once darkness set in the apparatus froze in place and was left until the next day. Miraculously, the damaged schooner was re-floated 12 days later and towed to New London.

The captain expressed his gratitude for the good work of the station crew in the following letter to the General Superintendent:

> "NEWPORT, R. I., *January, 1886. S.I. KIMBALL, General Superintendent U.S. Life-Saving Service, Washington, D. C.*
>
> DEAR SIR: *I wish to give expression to the gratitude I feel to the noble Service which you have done so much to promote, and which, during the late gale on the New England coast, so ably discharged the duty which men of the Service were called upon to perform, and more particularly to mention to your favorable notice Capt. H M. Knowles and his gallant crew of the Point Judith Station, Rhode Island. My vessel, the schooner Allen Green, of Providence, from Boston, Massachusetts bound to Baltimore, Maryland, was, by the hurricane of the 9th instant, in the midst of a thick snow storm, driven ashore about one mile to the westward of the above station, at 1.30 o'clock PM. and myself and crew of*

six men were compelled to instantly seek the rigging to escape the tremendous sea running at the time and making a clean breach over the whole length of the schooner. The rolling of the ice-coated vessel in the sea rendered our position most perilous. Within thirty minutes after we struck Captain Knowles and his crew, with their mortar cart, were at the scene and a line was shot across, the breeches-buoy rigged, and the struggle to bring us frost-bitten, ice-covered men ashore begun, which took until sunset, by reason of everything being covered with ice as soon as the water struck it. But the unremitting labor of Captain Knowles and his brave men brought us through at last. I have since viewed the path by which they reached us with the mortar-cart, and how they could have pulled it through the snow-drifts over fences and stone walls and reached us in so short a time will always be a mystery. The hospitable care and kind attention which we received at Captain Knowles' station soon made the men comfortable, although I suffered much that night from cramps and pains caused by the bruises I received before I went ashore, having been at the wheel fifteen hours continuously, the vessel being in ballast and steering very badly. But the kind attention of Captain Knowles mitigated very much my suffering. I was further agreeably surprised to be able to send the news of my disaster and safety to friends and owners, Captain Knowles putting in use the telegraph in the station, with the use of which I discovered he had made himself proficient in order to aid the Service in case of need, although out of the line of his duty, the signal officer formerly stationed there having been some time since removed. I cannot commend Captain Knowles too highly *for the kindness and courtesy shown us. The evident pride he has in making his a model station, the comfort realized there by myself and crew, and his efficiency in this valuable Service will be among my lasting memories. I remain, yours truly,*

ARTHUR L. NICKERSON, *Master Schooner Allen Green"*

1886 The Event of the Steamer *Miranda*

A somewhat strange occurrence involving the intentional flooding of a large ship took place June 20, 1886 when the British steamship *Miranda* of the Red Cross Line stranded 300 yards off the beach at Point Judith at 10:00 AM. *Miranda's* navigator misjudged the distance they were running off the beach and in clear weather found the vessel hard aground. *Miranda* was coming from New York in route to Nova Scotia and Newfoundland with cargo, crew and 40 passengers. There was no prospect of getting any of the cargo or people off the ship. The Point Judith Life-Saving Station was closed for the summer; but Keeper *Knowles,* with little delay, launched a small boat and pull up beside her. By sunrise of the next day *Knowles* had helped the passengers to get their baggage ashore and hosted them at the station where most of them secured transportation to Narragansett Pier. The report stated "many elderly ladies were exhausted and given cordials from the medicine cabinet". Milk was obtained for the children from a local farmhouse, and *Knowles'* wife provided hot meals. (Incidentally, Mrs. *Knowles* was one of the daughters of Point Judith Lighthouse keeper, *Joe Whaley*.) For the second time that year *Knowles* expertly operated the station telegraph system and transmitted messages for Captain *Edward Bindon* and his passengers. The following morning, *Miranda* started pounding on the bottom and Captain *Bindon*, alarmed that the vessel would begin to break up, intentionally flooded compartments in the ship to stabilize her. The crew and their baggage were brought ashore by *Knowles'* men who had been summoned as the sea conditions deteriorated. The next day oxen hauled the station's lifeboat to the site. The lifeboat was launched successfully and the ship's captain and carpenter flooded the last compartment and abandoned ship. One week after the *Miranda* stranded (July 27) she was pumped out, re-floated and towed to Newport.

In appreciation of Keeper *Knowles* and his crew's work, Captain *Bindon* wrote on July 16, 1886 to the Life-Saving Service General Superintendent:

> *"I received such valuable assistance from Keeper H.M. Knowles of the Point Judith Life-saving station, that I desire to return thanks for myself and crew for the services rendered. Within half hour after my ship went ashore, Keeper Knowles notified me personally that he was ready to render me every assistance. I proceeded to land my passengers forty in number and he piloted my boats to a safe landing through heavy breakers without accident. On the 23rd I abandoned the steamer, a heavy southeast gale blowing at the time and the keeper took the crew ashore and attended to our wants. He was the most cautious in putting me aboard and taking me ashore while a heavy and dangerous sea was running. I am sure had it not been for Keeper Knowles some accident might have occurred in landing the passengers as the beach is a difficult one to approach without the guide of a competent pilot. The*

surfmen were unceasing in their attention to the passengers and crew, working hard to do all that was needed. I feel it is my duty to place our testimony to these facts on record."

1887 The Event of the *Mary Natt*

Just past 3:00 PM on December 1, 1886 the station crew of the Point Judith Station observed the schooner *Mary Natt* acting in a strange manner and headed for land. Responding to a signal made on board, the surfmen manned a lifeboat and pulled towards her; but before they could get to the schooner it had run ashore. The *Mary Natt* of New York was bound for Somerset, Massachusetts with a cargo of pig iron and a crew of five men. She had sprung a leak and the captain was obliged to beach the schooner. The surf was too high to land safely with schooner's lifeboat. The men and their personal effects were brought off by the life-saving crew, taken to the station, and provided with medical attention and a hot meal. The following day the keeper secured free transportation for the crew of the *Mary Natt* to travel to Providence. Four days after grounding the vessel broke up into pieces and was a total loss. Wreckers later salvaged the cargo.

1887 The Event of the Schooner *Harry A. Barry*

In 1887 the large three-masted schooner *Harry A. Barry* of New Haven, Connecticut went ashore 400 yards south of Point Judith Station during misty weather. It was early morning (4:00 AM) and the ship was bound from Baltimore, Maryland for Fall River, Massachusetts with a cargo of coal and a crew of seven men. Although a high sea was running with only a light northwesterly breeze, the vessel was a total wreck. The life-saving crew reached the scene less than 30 minutes after the *Harry A. Barry* had struck shore, but heavy breakers made it impossible to get a boat alongside. Keeper *Knowles* called to the captain to stay aboard until daylight because of the great danger of the surf. However, one sailor heedless of the advice, place himself into the ship's yawl and was washed overboard by a giant sea and carried toward shore. The life-saving crew hurried along the shore to find him, and found him rescued by the station's cooks. The crewman, exhausted and nearly drowned, was revived. Meanwhile *Knowles* had decided to deploy the breeches buoy, since the vessel was beginning to break up. As they brought the apparatus along the beach and were preparing the gear, the sea began to subside allowing launching of the lifeboat. The life-saving crew took off one man at a time to the safety of the station where the Women's National Relief Association provided dry clothing. Later that afternoon, the life-saving crew returned to the ship with the captain in order to obtain a number of valuables that had been left on board. The following day the schooner broke up and was abandoned to wreckers. Two weeks later all the wreckage was sold at auction.

On March 17, 1887 the following communication was received by the Superintendent's Office:

"*Hon. Sumner I. Kimball*

Dear Sir,

On the 20th of February, the schooner Harry A. Barry, which I commanded at the time was run ashore on Point

Judith by the mate. The surf was very heavy when we struck, at times breaking over the vessel. The vessel struck at 4:10 AM, but so perfect is the system of discipline which you as chief of the service have established that, notwithstanding the darkness, we were discovered immediately and the glare of the Coston light, backed by the good record of the Service flashed hope to us all. The life boat was rowed out through the surf, backed down to us as near as the surf would permit, and the keeper told us to remain by the ship until daylight and then take us off. All this occurred within 30 minutes after we had struck. Everything would have gone well but my crew panicked and against directions of the keeper, launched the yawl-boat. It was soon capsized and one man was hurled by the surf to shore. The life savers rowed to shore, resuscitated the sailor and returned to the wreck and saved us all. We remained at the life station for several days receiving every attention. I have frequently read the feats of daring performed by your heroic men and I think my crew and myself owe our lives to the heroism of the Point Judith life-saving crew, the promptness of which I consider is due in a great measure to the efficiency of the General Superintendent of the Life-Saving Service.

Gratefully Yours,

C.W. Chatfield, Late Master of Schooner Harry A. Barry"

1887 The Event of the Schooner *Mary A. Drury*

On the last day of the year, December 31, 1887, the three-masted schooner *Mary A. Drury* of Boston, Massachusetts was bound for Providence with a cargo of soft coal and a crew of eight on board. The ship stranded at 4:00 AM on the end of Point Judith, a quarter of a mile north of the station. The weather was clear with a moderate westerly wind and the accident occurred due to an error of judgment in standing in too close to the land. The beach patrolman discovered the vessel immediately after she struck. He quickly flashed a Coston signal and then ran to the station and summoned the life-saving crew. The latter lost no time in manning the lifeboat, and ten minutes after launching they were alongside the schooner. The task of floating her was commenced at once, the surfmen helping to utilize all available canvas, and to work the pumps. At 7:00 AM the schooner floated clear with four feet of water still in the hold. The pumps were kept constantly going, sail area was increased, and every effort was made to get the craft to a harbor; but the water gained so rapidly she was run ashore again to prevent her from sinking. Captain *Knowles* telegraphed Newport for aid and in the afternoon a force of wreckers arrived, but easterly weather set in accompanied by a rough sea and they were obliged to abandon their operations with little progress towards freeing her. The life-saving crew remained on board and during the night assisted the crew to land with their baggage, and gave them comfortable quarters at the station. The next day (January 1) a heavy southeast gale prevailed and the schooner began to break up. People in the neighborhood gathered a large quantity of the wreckage. On January 2 the keeper assembled a team and conveyed the sailors and their effects to Narragansett Pier. They were given free passage after explaining their situation to the railway officials. The captain deferred his departure until he could settle up the business pertaining to the wreck. He stayed at the station until January 11 when he sold the materials saved by the wreckers and life-saving crew at auction, and disposed of the hull containing the cargo in a private sale.

1888 The Event of the Schooner *Earl P. Mason*

On August 22, 1888 the three-masted schooner *Earl P. Mason* with a crew of seven was bound for Boston, MA from Newport News, VA loaded with 700 tons of coal. The weather was so furious off Montauk Point that the captain of the schooner changed course for the shelter of Dutch Harbor in the West Passage of Narragansett Bay. Winds had increased and a change in wind direction caused the vessel to be stranded on the beach 1½ miles north of the station. Since the Life-Saving Service was on the summer schedule, only the keeper, Captain *Knowles*, manned the station. He and a young boy, *Leonard Webster*, manned a fishing boat, broke over the breakers and reached the *Earl P. Mason*. The schooner was taking on water and *Knowles* realized he could not bring the crew safely back to shore, so he towed their yawl into calmer waters. Meanwhile the keeper of the lighthouse at Point Judith contacted the LSS at Narragansett Pier where Captain *Allen* and two men commandeered a catboat, picked up the *Mason's* yawl and transported the crew to Newport. The *Earl P. Mason* was eventually floated, repaired and continued in service until 1912.

1888 The Event of the Schooner *Isaac H. Borden*

The *Isaac H. Borden* was bound for Providence from New York on September 9, 1888 laden with a cargo of kerosene. Burdened with a heavy sea and strong flood tide, the ship was thrown off course and onto the rocks three miles north of the Point Judith Station. The night surf patrol discovered her, fired off a Coston light and then returned to the station to summon the crew. The Narragansett Station was also summoned by Keeper *Herbert M. Knowles* to bring the beach apparatus, while the Point Judith crew would attempt to reach the schooner by surfboat. After a hard pull, the surfmen reached the vicinity of the *Isaac H. Borden* and boarded her, lowering her mainsail while attempting to keep their surfboat from being stove in by the rocks. They safely removed the three crewmen of the schooner and, with the help of the newly arrived Narragansett crew, hauled the surfboat and all those aboard up on the beach. The next day part of the cargo was removed by wreckers and the schooner broke up into pieces. The sailors were sheltered at the Point Judith station for four days before they secured passage back to New York.

1891 The Event of the Schooner *A.H. Hurlburt*

The disaster of the three-masted schooner *A.H. Hurlburt* in 1891 involved both the Point Judith and Narragansett Pier Stations. It occurred on the day after Christmas in 1891 when the 263-ton vessel with a crew of six men tried to reach the safety of Newport Harbor to escape a screeching gale force snowstorm. It was bitterly cold with a dangerous sea rolling in from the east and winds estimated at 60 mph. The ship was loaded with 400 tons of ice and bound for New York from Belfast, Maine. The *Hurlburt* missed the Brenton Reef Lightship, and midway between Narragansett Pier and Point Judith a crewman shouted "breakers ahead". Rounding up, the schooner dropped her anchors short of the rocky shore.

Both shore patrols of the Narragansett Pier and Point Judith Stations saw her predicament and hastened to their stations through deep snow to summon the crews. The Narragansett surfmen were already in the process of rescuing people from another wreck, the *Bill Stowe* four miles away.

Before assistance could arrive, the schooner parted her cables, was driven ashore upon the rocks, her masts fell and she began to go to pieces. The crew had no choice but to jump into the sea. The mate jumped first, missing the mizzenmast and was thrown under it by the breakers. He clung to a cake of ice and was pulled from the water by a local cottage resident. The captain and the cook also jumped, and were washed over the rocks into the surf. The captain was struck by a piece of timber and thrown under the ice and drowned. The cook just disappeared under floating timber and ice. Their bodies were discovered the next day, disfigured from the brutal beating of the surf and floating debris. Four others were saved.

Meanwhile, the *Bill Stowe* was aground on the rocks at Black Point to the north and the crew was desperately trying to get ashore safely. *H.M. Knowles*, the District Assistant superintendent, redirected the Point Judith crew to Black Point. They bundled the beach apparatus into the beach cart and replaced the water-soaked gear with dry apparatus from the Narragansett Station. The snow was flying so thick that visibility was very limited. Deep snowdrifts on the rough roads coupled with the heavily loaded cart slowed the crew from reaching the disaster scene in a timely manner.

1893 The Event of the Schooner *East Wind*

The exact location of the wreck of the schooner *East Wind* was not recorded, but on February 10, 1893 the crew of the Point Judith Station rescued the four-man crew after a hard and dangerous pull to windward in the station lifeboat. She was bound for Providence with a load of lime and encountered a strong southeast gale. The ship's crew was boarded at the station for a week. During that time their personal effects were brought ashore, and the vessel stripped for the owners before she finally broke up.

1894 The Event of the Sloop *Jennie*

As with many other incidents of strandings, this one also had a happy ending since the vessel was floated free. The unusual a part of the story was its cargo.

The sloop *Jennie* had stranded during fog on May 6, 1894 and had two feet of water in her hold. The two men on board were drenched and brought into the station, given food and dry clothes. The station crew returned to the *Jennie* and proceeded to unload 9,000 bricks to lighten her, then ran out anchors, pumped her out and floated her free.

1895 The Event of the Barges *Eagle, J.J. Naulty, Crocus, Albert M, and Beagle*

On January 26, 1895 the large ocean going tug *Sea King*, with a tow of five coal-laden barges, was bound for Providence from Long Island Sound in light winds. Within six miles of Point Judith the ship encountered a southeast gale accompanied with strong running seas and blinding snow. Weather conditions resulted in reduced visibility, making it impossible to see the towed barges. Breaking seas began to flood the tug. The master of the tug, Captain *Olmstead,* and the pilot on board decided to head off shore for the next seven hours. With daybreak they saw that the tow had broken apart and the barges were drifting and foundering. The closest barge was still attached to the tug and beginning to go under when they cut the towing hawser in an act of self-preservation. Twelve lives on board the five barges were lost, and only one man and one boy on the barge *Naulty* were picked up alive. Four women who were the wives and a daughter of the masters of the barges were among those who died.

The disaster took place too far off shore to be seen by the Point Judith beach patrol, particularly with the reduced visibility in the snowstorm. They later assisted in looking for bodies.

1898 The Event of the Steamer *Lewiston*

With heavy fog on September 5, 1898, the 234-ft steamer *Lewiston* was on her way to Boston from Montauk Point when she collided with the Point Judith breakwater. She had on board 149 passengers comprised of sick soldiers, doctors and nurses, plus a crew of 52.

The station crew heard the distress signals and launched the surfboat. They laid a plank from the *Lewiston* onto a lighter lying inside the breakwater. The passengers walked off the vessel onto the lighter that was then towed to Newport by a tug. There was much concern for the many ill men who were exposed to the inclement weather on the open deck of the lighter. The master engaged a tug to pull the ship off the rocks. The surfmen ran a line from a tug, pulled her off and brought her around inside the breakwater. The crew of the *Lewiston* re-boarded her, but she was leaking so bad they decided to drive her up on the beach under her own power. The following morning the surfmen transferred the crew onto the beach and then transported them to Wakefield. The keeper stayed aboard the vessel until a wrecking outfit arrived three days later. The steamer was repaired enough to be towed to Providence for complete repairs.

1898 The Event of the Schooner *Earl P. Mason*

This particular event is unusual primarily because it took place over a five-day period in August, when the station was in its inactive season and the regular life-saving crew was off duty. A very heavy southeasterly gale prevailed on August 22, 1898 and during its height, the three-masted schooner *Earl P. Mason* went ashore 1½ miles north of the Point Judith Station. The schooner was out of Providence and bound for Boston, Massachusetts from Newport News, Virginia with a cargo of coal and a crew of seven men. When she came ashore, heavy seas were breaking over her. The crew, fearing for their safety, launched the schooner yawl, not knowing that the fierce breakers would capsize their boat. The keeper of Point Judith Station noticed the craft some distance offshore; and realizing their fatal mistake in making an attempt to land through the breakers, summoned a young man living nearby to help launch a very large seine boat. By almost superhuman efforts with imminent peril to both vessels, they succeeded in working their way against the wind and the sea, and in wet and exhausted condition reached the schooner's yawl. It was a heroic and fearless act.

The tide was rising rapidly and with no chance to land at the time, the keeper deemed it best to wait until the turn of the tide. Meanwhile, the keeper at the Point Judith Light drove to Narragansett Pier and engaged a large catboat to go to the rescue of both boats. They arrived on the scene and towed the boats to Newport. Over the next four days, with assistance of the Brenton Point keeper who was visiting in the area and a wrecking crew, they stripped the *Mason* of its sails and rigging conveying the goods through the breakers in the surfboat. Eventually the schooner was floated off and towed to Newport for repairs, having lost a third of her cargo.

1906 The Event of the Schooner *Lugano*

The *Lugano*, a 40-year old vessel, was a 174-ton schooner hailing from Portland, Maine and bound for New York with a cargo of laths stored on her main deck and in the cargo hold. There was a crew of five men aboard, including her captain, *Edmund Barter*.

The ship was overtaken on November 15, 1906 by a violent east northeast rain and hail storm accompanied with a heavy swell which drove her on the rocky shore of Point Judith. Winds were clocked at 55 mph on Block Island. She had been taking on water and was unable pump fast enough to stay ahead. The ship foundered off shore, but her cargo of laths kept her afloat until she hit the rocks. Captain *Barter* decided to seek refuge inside the Point Judith breakwater, but the ship was so waterlogged she would not respond to her steering wheel and struck 200 yards north of the Life-Saving Station.

The life-saving crew responded in 15 minutes and shot a line from the beach to the end of the jib boom. The vessel's crew secured the line and hauled in the breeches buoy hawser, but because the schooner kept creeping toward the beach from the force of the breaking seas, there was difficulty keeping the line taut. Added to that problem, the buoy stopped half way to the vessel because the whip line snagged around the hawser 20 feet from the schooner. Keeper *Tefft* decided to obtain a second reserve apparatus from the station, but before that took place, captain *Barter* told his crew "I am not going to wait any longer, you will all have to lookout for yourselves." He then seized a plank and leapt into the sea. The crew followed his example except the cook who remained in the rigging. Only two men came ashore amidst the debris and both were saved by Keeper *Tefft* and a local fisherman named *John Champlin*.

The beach was patrolled all night. By morning the masts had broken and the forward part of the schooner had fallen apart. The district supervisor stated that it was one of the most complete wrecks he had ever seen. The following morning the bodies of the mate, a seaman and the cook were found almost a mile north of the station.

1907 The Event of the Barges *Jennie* and *Ida*

Manned barges, of which most were coal carriers, were commonly passing Point Judith. In the early morning of December 30, 1907, two barges met their demise off Point Judith during a fierce gale. Overwhelmed by heavy seas, the barge *Ida* sank two miles offshore from the life-saving station, and its master miraculously launched the barge's dory and rowed ashore informing the station crew that he was towing another barge, the *Jennie,* who was anchored and was being swept by heavy seas and in danger of sinking. The vessel was not in view of the station's crew due to heavy rain and poor visibility, yet they launched the surfboat and rowed for 1 hour and 40 minutes against heavy seas to get to the *Jennie* two miles away. They rescued the master and his wife and safely brought them in behind the breakwater. A few hours later the *Jennie* broke her ground tackle and came ashore on the rocks 150 yards from the life-saving station. She broke up and was a complete loss.

1909 The Event of the Schooner *G.A. Hayden*

On April 15, 1909, the schooner *G.A. Hayden* was found stranded about 1¾ miles north northeast of the Point Judith Station. With rough seas and late evening light it was determined to be too rough for launching the surfboat, so the crew transported the beach apparatus to the site of the wreck. With the aid of the Milburn Light, they succeeded in getting the whip aboard on the second shot of the Lyle gun. With the apparatus rigged, the first of the crew was landed by the breeches buoy at 12:10 AM, and after four trips the last man came ashore at 12:45 AM. All of the crew were taken to the station and provided with food and dry clothing. They remained at the station for four days until transportation was arranged to get them home. The schooner was a total loss.

> DEAR SIR: I wish to express my gratitude to you and your crew for your timely rescue of myself and crew of the schooner *G. A. Hayden*, wrecked on April 15, 1909, about 2 miles from your station, and which was being fast pounded to pieces on the rocks by the heavy surf. We were safely landed in the breeches buoy, otherwise we should have been swept to death by the seas or lost by the fast breaking up of the schooner.
>
> My crew join me in thanking you for saving our lives and for the kind treatment we received while at your station. Mrs. Whalen and my daughter also join me in this expression of our gratitude.
>
> With best wishes for your further success,
> I remain, yours, faithfully,
>
> Capt. THOMAS WHALEN,
> *Master of Schooner G. A. Hayden.*
>
> Capt. AMOS P. TEFFT,
> *Keeper of Point Judith Life-Saving Station.*

1914 The Event of the Schooner *Luella Nickerson*

Recorded as one of the most daring rescues performed by the Service, this event involved getting two men off the Point Judith breakwater. The rescue was performed on December 7, 1914 after the 26-ton schooner *Luella Nickerson* dragged her anchors and was smashed to pieces against the breakwater in a violent storm of hurricane force. The two men on board had made it safely onto a pole at the end of the breakwater, a full mile from land. For more than an hour they were exposed to icy spray and fierce biting wind and became completely drenched.

The station crew launched their surfboat equipped with anchors and worked their way to within 300-400 feet of the breakwater wall, dropped two anchors and cautiously paid out the hawsers getting the surfboat within 40 feet of the men. Twice heaving lines were thrown but they fouled on the rocks and could not be dislodged. One of the schooner crew dashed down between waves, slid down the rocks and succeeded in securing one of the lines; but misunderstanding the keeper in the surfboat, tied himself to the pole. Signals were exchanged and the keeper demonstrated that they should tie themselves to the line and then jump into the sea.

Both men then at the proper moment worked themselves down the rocks and cast themselves into the water. In short order both were hauled into the surfboat, but the next step was to get up the anchors and move away from the wall without swamping the surfboat. Up to that time the entire crew of the surfboat had been constantly at the oars to keep the boat from being swamped. For the next five hours they held the boat under the breakwater unable to leave the protection from the wind and sea. At 2:00 AM a Navy torpedo boat saw their plight and towed the boat near shore, but unable to make a landing they remained on the torpedo boat overnight.

Chapter 9
Quonochontaug Station USLLS #57

Quonochontaug was nicknamed "Quonnie" or "Quon" for obvious reasons. Nothing remains of the station today other than a foundation ruin, the result of the 1938 hurricane. The location was on one of the beautiful barrier beaches in the state. The site located at 41° 19'50"N, 71° 43'10"W was situated between two salt ponds, Ninigret Pond (a National Wildlife Refuge) and Quonochontaug Pond, on the promontory of the seaward entrance of the Quonochontaug Breachway. The breachway was a narrow (150-ft wide) shallow entrance into Quonochontaug Pond and its harbor, and at that time was partially silted in. One report regarding the station refers to the "narrow outlet to the sea", which suggests the life-saving station was located alongside the breachway rather than on the shoreline. The latitude and longitude coordinates also place the site on the west side.

This location allowed the station's surfboat and lifeboat (which was launched from rails) secure protection from the ocean side surf. The depth of water reaching out into Block Island Sound, south of the life station and a mile from shore, quickly drops off to 100 feet. There was no long reach of sand at low tide. The beach was short and abrupt, allowing easy launch of boats, but a difficult trek in the soft sand for the nighttime beach patrol, or when deploying the beach apparatus. Beach patrols extended along each side of the station and thus required crossing the breachway on the eastern side in a small skiff.

9 Quonochontaug

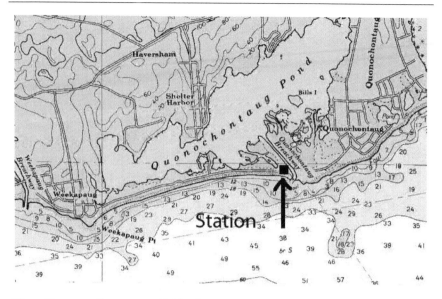

The Quonochontaug Life-Saving Station was built in 1891-1892 on a site "west twelve and three-quarter miles from Point Judith Light; east and 7½ miles of Watch Hill Light". It was extensively repaired in 1920. The station was listed as inactive in 1938 and disappeared from the records in 1939. Currently, the site sits vacant on an undeveloped lot inaccessible to the public, owned by the Quonochontaug Beach Conservation Commission (QBCC); and is one of the few remaining undeveloped, barrier beaches in Rhode Island. The QBCC is an umbrella organization of the Nopes Island Association, Weekapaug Fire District, Shelter Harbor Fire District, and Shady Harbor Fire District. The QBCC manages the area and apparently all of these organizations discourage use of the area by non-resident visitors and shore fishermen.

Breachway at the entrance of Quonochontaug Harbor in 2011. The Station was located across the water near this dune.   Photo by author

One angler called activities at the location "vigilante vandalism", referring to the practice of concealing boards with 3-inch nails in the sand along a sandy road that fishermen use to drive to the western side of the Quonochontaug Breachway.

The Quonochontaug Station house reached a level of fame as the model of 21 other life-saving stations along the east coast of the United States. The station's 1891 building design called Quonochontaug-type was replicated from 1892 through 1908 at other life-saving stations along the Atlantic Coast.

Designed by *George T. Tolman,* the Service's architect, the shingled buildings were one and a half stories high with a 10-ft wide attached boathouse and a hipped roof lookout tower where surfmen were posted in addition to the beach patrol. The Quonochontaug-type house was constructed at stations in Massachusetts, Rhode Island (Quonochontaug and Sandy Point on Block Island), New York, New Jersey, Maryland, Virginia, North Carolina, Florida, and a modified version on the Great Lakes in Illinois.

Keeper William F. Saunders

One of the 21 Quonochontaug-type Station houses constructed during 1892 and 1908 (Currituck Beach, VA 1903)   USCG Historian's Office

U.S. Coast Guard records concerning Quonochontaug are both sketchy and limited. Fortunately its first keeper, *William F. Saunders,* maintained a diary that is now archived in the G.W. Blunt White library at Mystic Seaport in Connecticut. Identified as the *William F. Saunders Collection* (Coll. 333), it covers the period 1872-1900 and provides a daily diary of the station, a daybook and other papers relevant to his responsibilities, including scrapbook clippings of related events not only at Quonochontaug, but also of other Rhode Island LSS stations. *Saunders* lobbied the service extensively to provide station keeper pensions. Previously a farmer and fisherman, he had eight children. *Saunders* started his career with the Life-Saving Service as a surfman at Station Watch Hill where he worked for three years before being promoted to keeper of the Quonochontaug Station in early December 1891. He served until November 1901, when he was found physically unfit to continue the position.

Other Keepers

Thomas T. Saunders succeeded *William F. Saunders* (December 14, 1901 until he resigned on December 18, 1905). *Thomas Saunders* was first stationed at Watch Hill in 1886. There is no information indicating if he was related to *William F. Saunders*. The next successors were *Howard Wilcox* (December 14, 1905 until his reassignment to the Watch Hill station on November 13, 1916), *George W. Streeter* (July 8, 1918 until reassigned to the Brenton Point Station on March 15, 1926), and *Albert Rohdin* (transferred from the Brenton Point Station on March 15, 1926, he served until he retired on November 17, 1928). Next, Chief Petty Officer *Arthur E. Larkin* is shown as being in charge in 1928; he was commissioned on October 10, 1930. He was reassigned to the Watch Hill Station on April 15, 1933 and was relieved by *Amos E. Broadmeadow*, who was reassigned from the Third District Office and served until his retirement on August 1, 1935. Next was *Arthur E. Larkin* (from the Old Harbor Block Island Station on January 17, 1936 until reassigned to the Point Judith Station on July 15, 1937).

Station Activation

Quonochontaug officially became operational on March 4, 1892 when the "colors" were raised. The station was equipped with a surfboat and a lifeboat, both mounted on rails for rapid launching. Crew training of seven surfmen began immediately, including breeches buoy deployment, surfboat and lifeboat drills, first aid and Lyle gun practice. Training with the Lyle gun was accomplished along the beach with a "practice mast" as a target. Training was repetitive and consistent. During the year 1899, 201 drills were conducted in four different categories.

DRILL	NUMBER CONDUCTED
Surfboat	45
Beach apparatus	53
Code signals	51
Resuscitation	52

9 Quonochontaug

The "Quonnie" Crew about 1885 Photo Saunders files

"U.S. Life Saving Station, Quonocontaug, R.I. [;] Howard P. Wilcox - Keeper, front right; George Tucker, 3rd from left; Bernie Sisson, center, rear row; Ed Champlin, center, front row"; dated as "about 1911"; photo numbered "MVF 972"; photographer unknown.

USCG Historian's Office

Surfman Herbert Levi Smith
Photo courtesy David Smith

An undated photo of the Quonnie crew with the station's cook.

In addition to the crew training, both the beach patrol and tower lookout had specific duties outlined in daily orders, and were required to report activities in their logbooks. The station was not active during the summer months of June and July. *Saunders* mentions in his diary that surfmen received increased salaries from $50.00 per month to $65.00.

From 1878-1889 the Quonochontaug crew experienced little change of personnel. In 1898 *Saunders'* diary lists the names of the following as being crew members over those years:

T.T. Saunders, C.A. Church, A.D. Sisson, E.E. Browning, Mortimer Lanphear, W.S. Gavett and A.T. Hoxsie.

In 1899 *E.S. Patter, H.L Smith* and *H.C. Dominy* replaced three members of the crew.

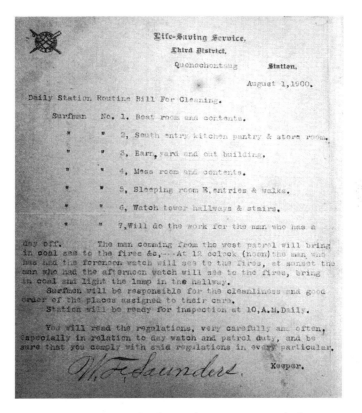

The *Saunders* papers include a description of the personnel and their mannerisms made by an unnamed reporter during an undated visit to the station:

> "Captain William Saunders has had charge of the station since 1892. No 1 was Thomas Saunders, a quiet fellow, who when he speaks, has a kind word for all. He has seen nine long years of service on the south shore and like his captain, he is a model in his line. He was one of the crew at Watch

Hill as early as 1886. On the other side was No 2 Charles Church a powerful man at age 26 years. He is a typical South County man who possesses all the skill, nerve and strength required in the line of duty. During his four years of duty he has passed through a number of hard tussles with the wind and wave, but he still guards his post in an efficient manner. No 3 was Amos Sisson a rugged fellow whose time of service extends over four years and like the others, his record is second to none in the service. No 4, James Sisson, the man who sculled the visitors across the breachway. He is the lightest surfman of the lot, but he is a good man. He has only one year on the beach. No 5, Mortimer Lanphear the musician at the station, who would make a good partner for Prof Moore of this city playing the banjo. For three years he has been on the roll of the station and without him life would be monotonous for the rest of the crew, although the cook (William Lanphear) is something of a banjo player. Between the watches the two Lanphears pick up their instruments and thus much pleasure is derived by the other fellows. William Gavitt No 6 always waits to keep company with the cook. It was when the station went into use that he was picked to be one of the crew. The last man was No 7 Asa Hoxie who in time of service ranks next to the Captain and surfman Saunders. Asa is known along the shore for at one time he watched the beach at Watch Hill and also at Point Judith. He was one of the men blown off shore and given up for lost a few years ago. Asa Hoxie is a man always in good humor, open frank in his manner and one upon whom the commander places great dependence in the hour when a vessel goes wrong as a few have on the treacherous sandy and rocky shore."

Selected Events Recorded in Annual LSS Reports (Modified for Clarity by the Author)

1893 The Event of the Schooner *John Paul*

A year after Quonochontaug Station was established, on February 11, 1893, the large four-masted schooner *John Paul* stranded during thick fog at Green Point. Found by the Quonochontaug Station beach patrol, additional help was summoned from Station Point Judith and Narragansett. A crew comprised of men from all three stations arrived on the scene with both the surfboat and the beach apparatus, but the master, captain *Whittier* and two crewmembers, a seaman and steward of the schooner, refused to leave the vessel. The weather was stormy and Keeper *Saunders* selected a crew of six to stand by at the scene of the wreck to maintain communication with the vessel and assist wreckers who were removing her cargo of coal during the following days. Pumps were put aboard in anticipation that she could be re-floated and they began pumping water out of her hull. In expectation of a worse case situation developing, Keeper *Saunders* rigged a line to the schooner.

Eight days later, on the 19th, a violent gale from the northeast set in with heavy snow creating 4-ft high drifts and by evening seas were breaking over her decks. The following morning the schooner was encrusted with ice and beginning to break up. The Quonochontaug crew spent three hours trying to launch their boat into the sea without success. The breeches buoy was not deployed because the men on board were incapable of securing the whip line. Finally, on the following morning, the surfmen reached the vessel and rescued the master and two crewmen. The *John Paul* was a total loss.

A letter of acknowledgement written February 21, 1893:

> "Dear Captain Herbert Knowles,
>
> I wish to congratulate you and the good work done by your men (Quonochontaug Station, RI) in rescuing the captain and two seamen from the schooner John Paul. They had a tough job to do acting like men all through it.
>
> Very truly yours,
>
> H.S. Bloodgood"

1898 The Event of the Sloop *Crocodile*

On October 3, 1898 at 8:00 PM during dense fog, the sloop *Crocodile* ran up on the rocks a half mile east southeast of the Quonochontaug Station. The station crew launched the surfboat and ferried the beach apparatus across the Quonochontaug Breachway. They arrived at the point opposite the wreck by 8:30 PM. She lay about 75 yards off shore, and on the first shot with the Lyle gun the line lay across the *Crocodile*. The crew set up the breeches buoy gear and safely landed two men from the wreck. The wreck then went to pieces and only several items of furniture were salvaged in addition to the lead ballast that was sold to a local wrecker. Below is the letter of acknowledgement from the *Crocodile's* master.

> HOBOKEN, NEW JERSEY, *October 26, 1898.*
>
> SIR: I wish to express my gratitude for the splendid behavior of the captain and crew of the life-saving station at Quonochontaug, Rhode Island.
>
> Unfortunately, on October 3, the sloop yacht *Crocodile*, of which I was in charge, was stranded about one-half mile ESE. of station on account of very dense fog then prevailing. Very soon the captain and crew from station came to our assistance, and in about one hour after stranding we were taken ashore and well cared for at the station. When I afterwards learned of the difficulties which had to be overcome before reaching the place of disaster, I could not very well realize how it could be done in such a comparatively short time. They must have worked as if their own lives were at stake instead of ours when they crossed the stream in front of the station building.
>
> * * * * * * *
>
> Congratulating you upon having such noble and active men at the Quonochontaug Life-Saving Station,
>
> I remain, yours, respectfully,
>
> THEODORE VAN BECK,
> *Master of Sloop Yacht Crocodile.*

1898 The Event of the No-Name Skiff

The daring event of a single-handed sailor resulting in loss of life is recorded in the May 3, 1898 report of the station. The station's surfmen recovered a 9-foot long skiff that a Captain *Crapo* used in an attempt to row from Providence to Cuba. He passed Point Judith at 6:00 AM the day before and was probably lost in the gale that sprung up an hour or so later. A month later, on June 3, the body of Captain *Crapo* was found washed up on the beach by a surfman.

1900 The Event of the Schooner *Nausett*

The loss of four lives of the crew of the schooner *Nausett* took place on January 27 or 28, 1900. Built in 1863, the 30-ton vessel was bound for Fair Haven, Connecticut from Providence with a cargo of oysters. On board were the Captain *Joseph Marques* and his crew of one, plus the captain's two young sons (ages 10 and 12).

The vessel's anchor light was sighted from Watch Hill Station the evening before and the following morning confirmed by Keeper *Davis* to be anchored in the middle of the channel called the Race. By noon, a strong gale had developed with wind speeds of 67 mph recorded at Block

Island and temperatures of only 16 degrees above zero. By darkness of the following day the schooner was no longer in view although the life-saving crew had kept a sharp lookout for her. The next morning the schooner was missing. Both life-saving stations, Quonochontaug and Point Judith were alerted, although *Davis* belicved she had run eastward to find a safe harbor.

At 8:00 PM, the eastern beach patrol reported a wreck 100 yards off shore east of the "key post" with more wreckage farther east in a location not covered by either the Watch Hill or Quonochontaug beach patrols. It was not until January 30 that the first body was found on Noyes Beach. The last body was also found there on February 4.

1902 The Event of the schooner *Kate and Mary*

During a west southwest gale on October 5, 1902 and in rough seas, the schooner *Kate and Mary* stranded close ashore 1½ miles east from the station at 4:00 PM. The station lookout promptly reported this and the crew launched the surfboat and pulled to the scene. They found the vessel fast aground and took her company of four men and the master's wife into the surfboat and landed them safely on the beach. They stayed at the station until the next day when the schooner was stripped of its spars and rigging and then abandoned. She had no cargo on board.

1906 The Event of the Sailboat *(unnamed)*

A letter (synopsized) dated July 8, 1906 and written by a Mr. *Robert Mooney* describes how his life was saved by surfmen from the Quonochontaug Station:

"My, Dear Sir, I take this opportunity to thank you as chief of the Life-Saving Service for the timely and valuable service rendered tom me by the surfmen and superintendent of the station in restoring my life on July 4. Three of us in a flat bottom sailboat capsized by jibing in a brisk wind and I was hit on the head by the boom, rendered unconscious pitching me under the sail and sinking me below the surface. A 17-year old member of our crew, Elisha Taylor, jumped in although he could not swim, grabbed me by the hair and brought me to the surface. I regained consciousness the following day where it was related to me about my narrow escape from death because of the services of your men.

Very truly, Robert Mooney"

1907 The Event of the Steamer *Larchmont*

This event, Rhode Island's worse marine disaster, is described in Chapter 1. It is included here in brief reference because the wreckage of the schooner that caused the disaster washed up near the Quonochontaug Station.

On February 12, 1907 when the schooner *Harry Knowlton* collided with the steamer *Larchmont*, the crew of the schooner abandoned the sinking vessel about 1½ miles offshore. She was blown ashore and sank ¾ mile from the Quonochontaug Station. Her crew of seven men came ashore in their yawl boat and were assisted by the surfman who was on the west beach patrol. They were brought to the station, given dry clothes from the Women's National Relief Association stores, fed and sheltered for the next two days.

Over the next few days, the schooner broke up and her remains washed up on the beach.

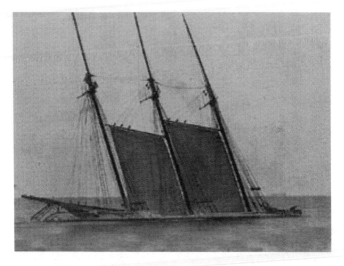

Three-masted Schooner Harry Knowlton ashore near Quonochontaug
Longo collection

1913 The Event of the Steamer *John B. Dallas*

On the night of October 12, 1913 the steamer *John B. Dallas* bound from New York to Block Island ran into a southwest gale and rough seas. She was loaded with coal and either because of shifting cargo in the heavy seas or stress of her hull joints she began taking on water. To prevent sinking, her master purposely ran her ashore two miles north of the Quonochontaug Station. At 7:00 PM she was discovered steaming close off shore by the station's watch lookout; but before a warning signal could be burned, the ship disappeared from view without coming any nearer to land.

The surfman having the 9:30 PM to midnight watch was sent out earlier than usual with instructions to keep an eye out for the steamer. At 9:35 PM he found her ashore and returned back to the station with the news of his discovery.

The station crew then dispatched the surfboat and breeches buoy apparatus to the scene. When they arrived the vessel lay 150 feet from the beach shore. The Lyle gun was used to fire a line across her that was immediately secured by the vessel's crew. The breeches buoy was rigged and with 15 minutes of the apparatus being set up, the crew of five was safely landed ashore. The *John B. Dallas* was a total loss with only part of her cargo saved.

9 Quonochontaug

Chapter 10
Green Hill Station USLSS #56

Green Hill Station, as did Quonochontaug Station, sat on the south shore of Rhode Island along the state's most spectacular stretches of sand. Today, to the delight of local bathers, they remain pristine waterfronts.

According to the U.S. Life-Saving Service annual reports, the Green Hill site was selected in 1907. The following year the title was secured. In 1910, "advertisement was issued for proposals for the construction of the station, but the single proposal received up to the date set for opening bids was deemed excessive, and a second advertisement has been published." Finally, in 1912, the station was completed and put in commission. The early position for the station was given as "west six miles of Point Judith Light". The station was listed as discontinued subsequent to 1934 and disappeared from the records in 1939. The property was turned over to the GSA for disposal in 1954.

Green Hill in Wakefield was purposely located 7 miles to the west of Point Judith in accordance with the requirement to have stations close enough together for surfmen from adjacent stations to patrol the entire beach and look out for vessels needing assistance. However, the Green Hill Station was bounded on each side by natural water barriers, limiting the watch area to 4.5 miles to the east as far as the settlement of Jerusalem situated at the west entrance to Point Judith Pond. To the west of the station, just over 2 miles away, lay the inlet to Ninigret Pond and East Beach that is now a state beach.

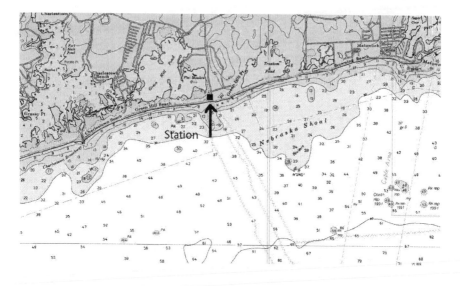

Today, nothing remains identifying station. A small parking lot and public access to the water at the end of Green Hill Beach Road, the exact latitude and longitude position (41° 20'23"N, 71° 36'00"W) identified by the USCG, is an open lot. Surrounded by beach grasses and a ring of summer cottages, some local residents claim the life-saving station was actually at the end of Coast Guard Avenue three streets to the east. One local resident claims the station was located at the end of Green Hill Avenue and that a house still standing there was at one time joined to the station.

Green Hill Station location per latitude and longitude coordinates in 2011
Photo by author

Disaster events recorded at the Green Hill Station are few, partly because annual LSS reports were discontinued in 1913. The station's first year activities had only one major incident significant enough to be reported in any detail. The 1912 report list only two incidents at Green Hill Station:

"Aug 19 ... ¾ of a mile east of the station: Schooner B.L. Tay, 150 tons from Bangor Maine" (see details below)

"September 15 ... 3 miles SW of station; Steamer Amanda F. Lancruft, 155 tons from New Haven". There was no further information on this incident.

During the next three years under jurisdiction of the U.S. Coast Guard, annual reports were consolidated and do not show any maritime events occurring at Green Hill Station. The station was in operation for 22 years and incidents are sure to have occurred, but the logs of this station have yet to be researched.

Keepers

The first keeper of the Green Hill Station was *William F. Hooper*, appointed on April 29, 1912 and retiring on August 16, 1928. He was followed by *Eli Sprague*, Jr. (reassigned from the New Shoreham Station on February 21, 1928 and reassigned to the Block Island Station on April 15, 1933).

Green Hill Station

USCG Historian's Office

Selected Events Recorded in Annual LSS Reports
(Modified for Clarity by the Author)

1912 The Event of the Schooner *R.L. Tay*

This was the first documented rescue performed by the life-saving crew of Green Hill Station and took place shortly after the station was operational in 1912.

The event took place on August 18, 1912 when the lookout at the station discovered the 151-ton lumber laden schooner *R.L. Tay* from Bangor, Maine bound for New York in distress. The weather was blowing a southwest gale and the schooner was running before it with her colors in the starboard rigging displayed "union" down (an earlier international signal signifying distress).

The *R.L. Hay* appeared to be coming ashore and the life-saving crew set out with their beach apparatus to intercept her where they thought she would strike. However, five minutes after they left the station the schooner was seen to anchor at a point ¾ of a mile east of the station and ¼ of a mile off shore. When this was observed, part of the station crew returned to the station and launched the Beebe McLellan surfboat to attempt to reach the schooner by boat rather than attempt an improbable long-range breeches buoy rescue.

After numerous attempts where the surfboat was filled with water and flung back on the beach, the surfboat reached the vessel and took off the crew of five men. However, weather conditions were so severe they were unable to return to the Green Hill Station and were obliged to take refuge in Point Judith Pond. Later when the storm had subsided they worked the schooner safely into Newport Harbor.

Chapter 11

The RI Volunteer Life-Saving Service

Rhode Island's U.S. Volunteer Life-Saving Corps

"It is the sacred duty of every normal person today to know how to save a life in the water."

George E Gross 1916

During the period the U.S. Life-Saving Service had deployed the nine maritime related surfside stations along the southern coast of Rhode Island, another needed organization emerged with fundamentally the same mindset. The difference was to provide humanitarian life-saving services for those who found themselves in danger of drowning in the state's bays, rivers and lakes.

Swimming had become fashionable by the late 1800s both as a recreational pursuit and as a means to escape the torrid summer heat. Resorts were being built and many beaches were equipped with bathhouses, cabanas, food concessions and family entertainment. Swimming or "bathing", as it was known, increased substantially, and along with it the occurrences of drowning. By the early 1900s, according to the American Red Cross, as many as 9,000 people nationwide drowned each year.

It was a call to duty and local organizations sprung up, most all of which were staffed by "life-saver" volunteers. They served as "life guards", a term much later used to describe their duties. At locations where no personnel were assigned, some apparatus such as a life ring buoy, float buoy and patrol boats were installed at docks, wharfs, pools and beaches. The buoy was provided for by anyone who witnessed the need of help to a person in the water and in danger. By the early 1900s methods of rescue and resuscitation similar to the British Royal Life-Saving Service were practiced and employed. The Young Men's Christian Association (YMCA) began its program of instruction in swimming and life-saving in 1907. The Boy Scouts of America followed shortly thereafter, and in 1914 the American Red Cross established a national program of life-saving and water safety.

The various life-saving services intermingled, such as the United Volunteer Life-Saving Corps, The American Red Cross Life-Saving Corps, U.S. Lifeguard Service, U.S. Volunteer Life-Saving Corps and the National Life-Saving Service. At local levels additional organizations were created with various names, all chartered toward the same purpose.

Commodore *Wilbert E. Longfellow*

Rhode Island began its involvement in life-saving due to the efforts of one young man *Wilbert E. Longfellow.* As a reporter for the *Providence Telegram* he covered the State House in Providence. He had joined the Volunteer Life-Saving Corps and began assisting in the patrol and lookout at various state beaches and at the same time demonstrating and training others in life-saving techniques. It has been said that for a large man he had boundless energy, and with a loud voice and entertaining nature he campaigned for water safety and funds to be provided at beaches throughout the state. Every municipality in the state enthusiastically endorsed his conviction that life-saving was an inherent need at Rhode Island beaches.

He was successful with the Rhode Island legislators and within a few short years he had reduced the state's drowning rate by 50%. By 1906 he had become the Rhode Island State Superintendent of the U.S. Volunteer Life-Saving Corps lobbying for a budget of $1500, $1200 more than the $300 he was allocated in the previous year.

RI State Superintendent Longfellow in 1907

Ten years later in 1916 the American Red Cross liked his ideas and mannerism so much they hired him as their national director where he established the Red Cross Volunteer Life-Saving Corps. That too being successful, *Longfellow* traveled from community to community, training and recruiting good swimmers and the organizing them into volunteer units. Policemen, Boy Scouts and YMCA members were all part of this national movement. Certificates were awarded and over 1,000,000 instructors have taught water safety practice to millions of others. His motto "Every American a swimmer, every swimmer a lifesaver." was carried along with him as he promoted the virtues of waterproofing life-saving. Throughout the country under his direction death rates from drowning plummeted downward dramatically. His success earned him the title of Commodore in Chief of the U.S. Volunteer Live Saving Corps from the Red Cross. He passed away on March 18, 1947 three months after he had retired.

Wilbert Longfellow in his later years with the Red Cross Life-Saving Corps. Because of his size and swimming skills he was nicknamed "The Whale."

The Rhode Island Units

The first annual report (1906) to the General Assembly of Rhode Island was compiled by *Longfellow* and identified the organization as the U.S. Volunteer Life-Saving Service Corps (USVLSC), Department of Rhode Island. The report highlights sixteen rescues that occurred during the past year by members of the Corps. The Corps numbered 300 volunteer members organized in 60 crews. Two years later the volunteer force numbered 500. Apparently this took some organization skills since the volunteers provided services that covered weekdays, nights, holidays and weekends with regular patrols established at the more populated beaches.

The state headquarters were located in Pawtuxet at a location called Oates Block. The state was broken up into districts and at each district a Lieutenant was assigned. Each district in turn was identified by location where services were provided or equipment was installed. In many cases several crews were assigned to a station with five men comprising a crew. By 1908 the USVLSC headquarters were moved to 1297 Broad Street in Providence.

Districts and Locations

Providence Harbor District: RI Co's Power House, City Bridges, Steamboat Docks, Narragansett Electric Lighting Company Power House, Pawtucket Boat Club, Pawtucket Water Works Repair Shop, Newell Coal and Lumber Co. Swimming Hole, Fields Point and Wharf

East Providence District: Three at Riverside, Barstows-on-theTenMile, Wonkituk Canoe Club, Silver Spring, Boyden Heights, Crescent Park Beach, Crescent Park Wharf

Pawtuxet District: Washington Park Boat Club, Kirwins Beach, Edgewood Yacht Club, Pawtuxet Cove, Three Stations, Rhodes on the Pawtuxet, Swastika Canoe Club,

11 The Life-Saving Corps

Pawtuxet Canoe Club, Brown Farm Summer Camp, Rock Island

West Shore District: Coles Camp Boat Club, Mark Rock, Shawomet Beach, Double Crew, Longmeadow, Rocky Point Bathing Beach and Steamboat Wharf, East Greenwich Boat Shops

Bristol District: Warren Bridges, Bristol Yacht Club, Ferry Landing, Pappoosequaw Point, Bristol Ferry

Newport District: Long Wharf and both Beaches

Narragansett Pier: Sherry's Pavilion, Taylor's Bath, Broad Walk, Casino Slip

Other: Westerly-Wickford, Two Stations, Prudence Island, Two Stations (not yet districted)

RI Volunteer Life-Saving Corps Images of The Past

Rocky Point Wharf USVLSC Crew
1907 Annual report

11 The Life-Saving Corps

Pawtuxet Cove Storage Shed

Demonstrating proper tying of life jacket.
Annual Report

Demonstration of the "bellows movement of resuscitation"
Annual Report

Corps Work Records Summary for Year 1907

Total Stations	131	
Rescues	12	(1904), 20 (1905), 51 (1906), 50 (1907)
Life buoys	59	Kapoe rings, 42 cork rings, 3 buoys
Medicine Chests	15	large metal cases

Bathing Dress

There was serious concern by the Life-Saving Corps concerning the appropriate bathing dress for women and girls. The common three-piece or heavy two-piece suits when wet were considered cumbersome and a serious impediment to swimming. Said *Longfellow*; "under the circumstances it is a wonderment that so many girls finally master the art of swimming". Even the "common sense bloomer suit" was considered a handicap, although some excellent swimmers hesitated to wear it in public and willingly doffed the superfluous skirt on entering the water. Most of the more popular beaches rented both men's and women's bathing suits.

A somewhat humorous yet gallant rescue was performed at Kirwin's bathing beach on August 11, 1907 when two life-savers rescuers saved a 200-pound man. The man's heavy wool water laden bathing suit dropped around his feet and he was unable to keep afloat. His inability to swim prevented him from keeping afloat and he would have drowned had not the life-saver on the Corps patrol boat been close by. The victim was pulled up clutching the neck of his rescuer, and a second life-saver jumped in to assist. The man was taken aboard the boat in serious condition, resuscitated and taken to shore after his "clothing was restored and fitted properly".

Membership

Membership certification in the USVLSC required proficiency in swimming skills, in addition to a number of related capabilities. After training candidates were tested and scored points on the various subjects in the test.

Subject *Points*

1. *Swimming not less than half mile for active members, 100 yards for auxiliary members, and 25 yards on the back for both* 10
2. *Diving, plunging, floating, fetching* 10
3. *Rescue drill on land and water* 10
4. *Release drill on land and water* 10
5. *Resuscitation* 10
6. *Names of parts of a rowboat* 5
7. *Rowing and boat handling* 10
8. *Use of life-saving appliances* 10

9. First aid work and remedies 10
10. Written examination on work in water 5
11. Written examination on work in boats 5
12. Written examination on work on land 5

(The applicant had to receive no less than six points on each ten point subject and not less than three points on five-point subjects.)

The Edgewood and Kirwin's Beaches

For over a thirty-year period the two most popular beaches were Edgewood and Kirwin's Beaches, located on Narragansett Bay. The beaches along Rhode Island's south coast were not readily accessible, except by automobile, and families did not commonly own vehicles as they do today. Edgewood and Kirwin's Beaches were both in the Edgewood suburb of Cranston, just south of the city line that separated Providence and Cranston. Their popularity was due to the proximity to Providence, and a convenient trolley line (5 cent fare) from downtown Providence that ended one block from the beaches. Both had bath houses and food concessions and pristine sandy beaches.

Edgewood Beach circa 1910
Annual Report

The Metropolitan Parks Commission secured Edgewood Beach in 1909 for $9,400 and included 11,000 feet of broad sandy shore. Fresh water lines were extended down to bathhouses and a concourse for carriages and automobiles was also constructed. The Life-Saving Corps established a station at both beaches with quarters and refreshment rooms.

The RIVLSC crew assigned to Kirwin's Beach 1910
Annual Report

Mr. *Edward Greer* of the Metropolitan Park Commissioners in 1909 wrote:

> *"Let anyone who desires an object lesson go to Edgewood Beach and think of the deprivation that our enormous industrial community would suffer if this surviving neighborhood playground, within the five cent fare of the city, were not saved as a natural resource. An investment in Edgewood Beach today is an investment in the future".*

By 1941 Edgewood and Kirwin's Beaches were history. World War II was almost upon us and both beaches were buried under a mammoth shipyard project to meet the wars demands.

11 The Life-Saving Corps

Bibliography

Brown, Dwight C. *Afloat on the Rocks.* Kettle Pond, August 2011

City of Wakefield, RI. *GIS Plat Maps and Land Records,* 2010

Claflin, James. *Lightships & Lighthouses.* Arcadia Publishing Company

Committee on Interstate & Foreign Commerce. *Congressional Report 1908*

D'Entremont, Jeremy. *The Lighthouses of Rhode Island.* Commonwealth Edition, 2006

Smith, David. *Surfman Herbert Levi Smith at Quonochontaug.* North Kingstown, RI

Georges's of Galilee. *Steamer Larchmont Life Raft*

Jenney, James. *Beavertail Lighthouse Museum Association Wreck Data Sheets.* 2007-2011

Karentz, Varoujan, *Beavertail Light Station.* Booksurge Publishing, 2008

Cooney LCDR, Fredrick. *Quonochontaug Discussions.* Charlestown, RI, August 2010

Goss, George E. *Life-Saving.* 1916

Bacon, Edgar Mayhew. *Narragansett Bay, Its Historic and Romantic Associations and Picturesque Setting.* Putnam, 1904

Narragansett Times. *Point Judith Vessel Tracking.* June 1872

New England Lighthouses website. *Point Judith Vessel Traffic.* December 2010

New York Times. *Schooner Randall.* December 29, 1911

New York Times Historical Newspapers (1857-1922). *Perils of the Surf,* 1877

Newport Mercury. *Various Issues*

Noble, Dennis L. *That Others May Live.* Naval Institute Press, 1994

Providence Public Library. *RI Volunteer Life-Saving Corps Annual Reports*

Livermore, Rev. S.T. *History of Block Island.* Lockwood & Brainard Co., 1876

RI Ocean Special Area Management Plan. *Chapter 4 SAMP draft.* July 23, 2010

Longo, Mildred Santille. *Picture Postcard Views of Rhode Island Lighthouses and Beacons.* Rhode Island Publications Society, 1990

Shanks, Ralph and Wood York. *The U.S. Life-Saving Service.* Costano Books, 1996

The U.S. Life-Saving Service Heritage Association (USLSSHA) website, *http://www.uslifesavingservice.org*

U.S. Coast Guard. *Annual Reports 1915-1920*

U.S. Coast Guard Academy Library and Museum, Groton, CT

U.S. Coast Guard Historians Office, Washington, D.C.

U.S. Life-Saving Board. *Annual Reports 1856 – 1914*

U.S. National Archives. *Category #26 Record Files.* Waltham, MA

Westerly Sun. *Larchmont Bodies 1902.* Feb 7, 1999. page 29

Saunders, William F. *William F. Saunder's Papers.* Collection 333. Mystic Seaport Library

Sisson, William. *Soundings.* July 2010

Wireless & Steam Museum. *Robert Merriam Massie Radio Station.* December 2010

Made in the USA
Charleston, SC
27 May 2014